June 20, 2014

Charles and Mary,

May you be richly
blessed in all that
you set your hand to!

[signature]

TRAILER

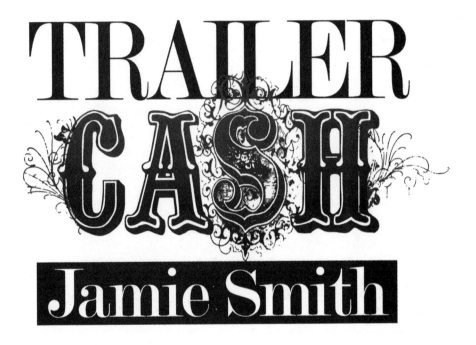

CASH

Jamie Smith

TRAILER

HOW TO CASH IN ON THE LOW-INCOME HOUSING INVESTMENT BOOM | LEARN THE KEYS YOU NEED TO SUCCEED!

HIGHERLIFE
DEVELOPMENT SERVICES, INC
Oviedo, Florida

Trailer Cash
by Jamie Smith

Published by HigherLife Development Services, Inc.
400 Fontana Circle, Building 1, Suite 105
Oviedo, Florida 32765
(407) 563-4806
www.ahigherlife.com

Cover Design: r2cdesign—Rachel Lopez

First Edition
11 12 13 14 — 9 8 7 6 5 4 3 2 1
Printed in the United States of America

Dedication

This book is dedicated to my incredible husband,

my most special gift.

Every day he inspires me to be the best version of myself.

Table of Contents

Introduction

As I look back a few short years ago, I was leaving college with two degrees and no intent to work in my field of study because I had a different plan. It is truly amazing how much can be accomplished in a short period of time. Today, my husband and I are blessed to be able to vacation wherever and whenever we want. However, one of the most rewarding parts of being financially successful is the ability to share our success with those we care about. Whether it's a BBQ at our lake house, a beach-side retreat at the Four Seasons in West Palm Beach, Florida, or a visit to South Africa on behalf of our foundation to serve those in need, spending time with the people we love is what life is all about, we've found. And that is what being financially successful gives you: it gives you time. At this point in my life, I'm where I want to be, doing what I'm called to do. I am satisfied. Despite the naysayers and the doomsday predictions against my career plan, I've made it. What's more, I can honestly say I'm happy—exceptionally happy.

Growing up, I did not have a financial role model. I saw my family and loved ones work very hard, but I also observed that they lived with a paycheck-to-paycheck mentality. One vein that runs strong in my family is an incredible work ethic, but the lack of financial guidance in their lives allowed for many long hours of work with very little to show for it. As I grew up, I saw the need for a plan that would allow for financial freedom, not only for myself but for my family as well. My business today is that plan.

While I didn't know at thirteen how today would come to be, I was searching. Searching for a path to financial freedom so that

1

I could have the ability to help others do the same. Much of my business plan is included in this book, and it is my sincere desire that your life be positively impacted through its pages.

Almost a decade ago, I lived in a hot, unfinished garage and worked several jobs while paying my way through college. Just as a sapling's roots take hold in the warm days of spring, the seeds for my plan took root in that hot, unfinished garage. My husband used to joke that if I ever came home late at night and hit the wrong switch, my wall would go up! And as funny as it sounds, it was the truth.

You may have picked up this book because you want to live more comfortably. Or perhaps you're looking for a way out of your current financial situation—a means to produce consistent monthly income for your family in this, or any, economy. If you are looking for a plan to create monthly income and long-term wealth, you've opened the right book. I have found financial success, and it is my desire that this book help you do the same. If you are willing to take the information provided in this book and apply it to your life in a similar fashion, there is no doubt in my mind that you will be every bit as successful as you desire to be.

Chapter 1

Someone's Making Bank— It Might as Well Be You!

I could say that my first epiphany concerning finances began at a Perkins restaurant. One Saturday morning, when my mother was out working one of her jobs, I was in the classic "home alone" scenario. My two younger brothers were with our dad for the weekend, and I was alone. I was thirteen—too young to work a regular job—so I scraped together all the change I could find and walked down the street to have breakfast at Perkins, a little diner on the corner. I had eaten at this restaurant before, but this one Saturday, as I sat in the corner booth, I felt pretty sorry for myself.

My family had always struggled to make ends meet. When my parents divorced when I was in the fifth grade, my dad left my mom with very little support and fought with her about paying even less. So my mom stepped up to the plate and worked even harder. As a kid, I thought the extra jobs would bring more leisure money, but somehow we never had much. My mom was remarkable. She did the best she could and certainly wasn't afraid of working to support us. Yet it seemed to me that morning at Perkins that nothing ever changed and nothing ever would. It hit me hard. My whole family worked hard—we just didn't have anything to show for it.

How does anyone ever get out of this cycle of being broke all the time? I wondered.

I didn't have a clue. All I knew was that I didn't want to spend the rest of my life feeling trapped and miserable like this. My desire was not so much for wealth as it was for independence. Even at thirteen, it was easy to see that financial success meant freedom. I wanted the freedom to not worry about money that I needed for school clothes, books, gas in the car to go places, and, well, breakfast at Perkins. In the back of that aging restaurant at an uneven table, I realized I needed a plan.

A statement that my mom used to make popped in my head: "If you're waiting on someone else, you're backing up."

It wasn't a lightning-bolt moment. It was just a simple realization that came over me during breakfast: *if I wanted something, no matter what it was, no one was going to do it for me.* No one, as the responsibility is only mine. The good Lord gave me two arms, two legs, a brain, and a heart to serve others—and those were, are, and have always been the foundation of my business.

> If you're waiting on someone else, you're backing up.

To an onlooker, it might have appeared that I was alone in that booth, but neither I nor you have ever been alone a single day in this world. My personal faith has provided me internal stability so that I could be externally focused. You may not be a person of faith, but there is no doubt that you were made to accomplish great things for the benefit of others.

Despite being raised in the church, I am not religious. I am, however, relational. At this point in my life, I realize that the value in everything is in a relationship. Faith is a relationship with your Creator. Marriage is a relationship with your spouse. A business is a relationship with your stakeholders.

You may, like my family did, have a relationship with money that is an endless loop of frustration—financial frustration. Looking back, my family could have clearly benefited from many of the principles taught through courses like Crown Ministries or Financial Peace University, but many churches choose to avoid the topic of finances in an attempt not to alienate their membership or create an uncomfortable environment. The failure of a church family, or any family, to openly discuss finances robs them of the blessing of being financial successful and the fruit that it bears—the fruit being the ability to give of your time, talents, and treasures.

At this point in my life, after giving numerous speeches and after meeting tens of thousands of investors, I find it encouraging that most of those I have met are driven more by what they can give than what they can accumulate for themselves. I also find it necessary to mention that I have found this almost innate desire has been held by atheists, Christians, Muslims, and more.

I was determined that my life was not going to be about sitting around waiting on someone else or complaining about everything I didn't have that other people did. I figured people either whine about their lives or do something to improve it. I already knew from hearing other people complain that complaining didn't help anything. So I made a decision in that moment—I refused to be a whiner. I would do whatever it took, within honest means, to make "it" happen.

When my mom got home that day, I told her, "You watch me, Mom. I'm going to make it big. And you're going big with me." She laughed and nodded her head. I meant it, and I think she knew I did.

Looking for That Opportunity

Preparation came to me during my childhood. But opportunity— I had to go out and find that. Through research, I learned that more millionaires had been created in real estate than through any other avenue. As I considered that, the desires of my youth, coupled with my newfound direction, produced opportunities that I began to see in the marketplace.

It's funny—just when it feels like you are about to be swallowed whole by the discouragement of not enough time, not enough money, or too much responsibility, an opportunity will present itself to the person seeking it. It's been said that luck is the intersection of opportunity meeting preparation. If you're prepared, you can see an opportunity in front of you and walk that opportunity into a deal that will change your life. That has definitely been true for me.

Perspectives Learned

As I have mentioned, one of the benefits of being successful financially is the reward of time. My husband and I found ourselves in our twenties with the ability to retire. I had a problem with that because in my family, retirement is called a funeral. We work, and we work hard. I find it intriguing that many Americans find themselves looking forward to retirement with very little idea of what they are going to do with themselves when they get there. I certainly can't speak for all people, but for me, sitting on a beach sipping a mai tai day in and day out is horribly boring and largely unfulfilling.

Years ago, I heard my husband's grandfather give his definition of a business, and I loved it. He said, "A business is providing a product and/or service that blesses the life of someone else in order to derive a profit." I thought it was a great picture of what a business is to do, and that is to serve. My husband always says, "You serve to make and give to keep." In any economy, you have individuals out to earn a penny on the backs of others. The problem is, that isn't a business. Simply put, starting a business with the sole intent to make money without leaving your customers better than you found them is a scam.

Don't misunderstand me. Money is a wonderful tool, but it is not the goal—rather, it is a byproduct of the goal, which is serving your customer. I find it ironic that many of those who chase money for money's sake never find it. I know many who have been extremely successful, well beyond their dreams, and I enjoy learning about how they go about their business each and every day. Many of them work well beyond five o'clock and start well before nine o'clock. Many of them work past the age of retirement. Why do they do this? Because it isn't about them! They are driven by a desire to do better and to do more for the benefit of others, and they are rewarded financially for it. At the end of the day, if you have, you can give. That doesn't mean you can't enjoy the benefits of having money, like driving a nice car, living in a nice home, or taking nice vacations, but to miss the blessing of being able to give is to miss one of the most precious gifts I have experienced to date.

In this book, we are going to talk plenty about making money, but it is important to first lay the ground rules. In this or any business, you must have a heart for serving your stakeholders, even if that means it takes longer for your success. This focus has not only made me a significant amount of money, but it also allows me to sleep at night. Money cannot buy a good night's sleep.

The "I Don't Have's ... "

There is a sound that is like fingernails on the chalkboard to me, and that is the sound of the "I Don't Have's..." I am blessed to have time, which is afforded to me by my business. Many years ago, my husband and I were invited to speak and teach groups of investors the fundamentals of our business and how we operate.

After prayerfully considering the invitation, we accepted, and we allocate a portion of our time to speaking and teaching today.

In each class we teach and work with, there is a portion of the crowd we deem the "I Don't Have's…" This designation has nothing to do with the capability of the student but rather the way their sentences always start when telling you why they can't become successful. For example, they say:

- I don't have good enough credit to start investing.
- I don't have enough money to start investing.
- I don't have the knowledge to start investing.

Food for thought: as I am writing this, there are over 7 million millionaires in the United States alone. The majority of millionaires were not born into wealth but, like myself, had to see an opportunity and work like mad to realize it. The fact is, every person who hasn't taken action has an excuse, while every successful person has seen the same challenges but has chosen to overcome them to be successful. Stop looking at the speed bump—get over it!

I realize you may wonder how you can get past some of your limitations, and so I have sought to list the most common objections that I have received from the "I Don't Have's…" over the years. They are as follows.

"I don't have credit."

This is a valid limitation but not a deal breaker. In future chapters, we will discuss seller financing and other financing alternatives that are still available to you with poor credit. I have purchased multiple properties where my credit score wasn't even a consideration. In addition to seeking alternative financing options, there are many things you can do to improve your score in a short amount of time. For a list of credit-repair resources, visit www.trailercash.com.

"I don't have money."

Not to be overly simplistic, but if you don't have any money, don't use it! I have learned that many who have no money have had it in the past, but it wasn't used effectively. See, if you have money and use it, you go back to having no money again. Those who have money typically choose to use it as infrequently as possible. My husband and I have been blessed to have more money today than we ever have before and we use less money now than ever before.

Think of it this way. If you had $100,000 and could buy a property that returns $20,000 in its first year, you would earn a 20 percent return on cash. But what if rather than investing your $100,000, you were able to use another source of funding (which we will discuss later) and you could earn an infinite return on cash? Which return would you prefer?

Now for the big question. Which return do you think pension-fund managers, banks, and the wealthy prefer? It's an interesting irony that while the wealthy do not typically use their own money, many times those who are poor use the excuse of not having money as the reason they can't get started.

"I don't have a high IQ."

Believe it or not, I have heard this one on a number of occasions. Success has nothing to do with a level of intellect. If that were the case, most millionaires would be engineers or some other such profession. The missing piece for most individuals isn't intelligence but rather a lack of competence. Competence acquired through an investment is applied knowledge.

Many Americans working in corporate America are actually more intelligent than their superiors. I saw this firsthand while interning in college for a major employer in the Orlando area. The problem, I quickly realized, wasn't an issue of intelligence but rather competence. See, people who are extremely intelligent can be overly confident that their intelligence is all they need to be successful. Oftentimes highly intelligent and/or successful individuals tend to believe that the success they have already achieved in a specific area will naturally correlate to success in other areas. Have you ever seen a former NFL athlete think he can become a successful real-estate developer just because he was a star athlete? There are many people like this, and they have lost their rear ends because they were not competent in the specific area of business they were trying to pursue. If you are not overly intelligent you can't "get smart," but you can gain competence by learning from and through those who have already done what you are looking to do. Once competent, you can set out to hire those who are far more intelligent but far less competent. In the end, intelligence works for competence.

"I don't have the knowledge."

Then get it! Only you know what you need to learn to get to the other side, so set out to find it and don't stop until you do. Knowledge is great to have, but it isn't everything. When you were in your mother's womb, did you study in order to obtain knowledge of how to breath? No! You came out, got spanked, and learned real fast.

The fact is, you will never know everything you need to know before taking that first important step. You must not only consider the risks in taking the step but—more importantly—the risks in *not* taking that first step toward your goal of financial success.

To repeat, I am not saying that you do not have challenges. Of course you do, and I still do today, too. But overcoming challenges is what builds confidence and allows you to overcome greater obstacles in the future. It is imperative that you focus on what you can do with what you do have so you can serve those who truly don't have.

Commercial vs. Residential

Before we dive into mobile home parks specifically, I feel it is important to state the case for multifamily commercial real estate compared to single family or multifamily residential real estate. You may be asking, "What is the difference between multifamily commercial and multifamily residential?" The difference is contingent on the unit size of the property. A property with four units (rentable doors) or less is typically considered residential. For instance, if you purchased a quadruplex, it would be a multifamily residential dwelling. That being said, if four units or less is residential, then five units or more would be considered commercial. For example, if you purchase a thirty-unit mobile home park, you would own a multifamily commercial property.

I often meet investors who want to "start small." It always makes me smile for this reason. I will usually ask someone who says that they want to "start small" how many properties they own. They typically respond with, "None." I am always careful to point out that if an individual has no investment properties, it would be impossible to start small! Simply buying one unit would represent an infinite growth over the number they previously held, which was none. That is to say, if you have nothing at present, you cannot start small—only infinite.

Many people with the desire to become a real-estate investor seek to purchase a single-family property with the hopes of moving into duplexes, then triplexes, then quadruplexes, and so on. There are many problems I see with that formula, the primary being time. As a rough average, you should be able to make $100 per door per month. If you purchase a single-family home, after all the expenses, you should make around $100 net (take home). You would be surprised how many times I meet individuals who say they are making $500 per month or more per unit, and when I begin to ask detailed questions about real-world expenses, they agree that they didn't factor for that. A property that brings in

$1,500 per month with a mortgage payment of $1,000 does not make $500 per month. Where were the management expenses, vacancy, credit loss, and so much more?

So, given $100 per month per unit you own, you would have to purchase thirty single-family properties to make roughly $3,000 per month. If that excites you, then go for it, and you will have no competition from me! See, if I could purchase a thirty-unit mobile home park, I only have to buy one property to make the same $3,000 per month as you.

What Is This All About?

As my good friend Zig Ziglar has said me, "When you get to the top, send the elevator back down and bring others up to enjoy the view." That speaks of a relationship. There have been many studies that show an individual will survive longer for the benefit of someone else than they will for just themselves. We are made for relationships!

I have been fortunate to learn from so many brilliant people, but none more brilliant than my friend and pastor Dr. Joel Hunter and his gifted wife, Becky. It was years ago when I heard Pastor Hunter teach that, "True love seeks an object," and I have never forgotten it.

What is motivating you to read this book? I hope you have a sincere desire to become financially free by serving those around you. But more importantly, I hope you can begin to see what a difference you can make for your family, your church, your charity, and so many more. Never forget them. They are who you are serving everywhere and every day. If you lose this focus, you will lose your business.

Chapter 2

Why Mobile Home Parks?

In my experience, nothing brings humor to an introduction like telling people that you own mobile home parks. My husband and I were recently at a wine festival in Steamboat Springs, Colorado. During the course of an evening, I found myself in a conversation with a group of uppity-yuppity women—straight out of *Sex and the City*—and when they inquired as to what I did for a living, I proudly replied that I own mobile home parks. I was like Pepé Le Pew amongst a field of roses.

All jokes aside, one question that I am commonly asked is, "Why mobile home parks?" I can give you a thousand answers to that question, but the most simplistic is that it just makes sense. On a macro level, the demand for low-income, affordable housing in our market is on the rise, largely because of its low cost. Name a city that doesn't have a demand for quality, affordable housing. When do you think that will change?

An opportunity that jumped out at me from the outset was the lack of quality housing in the low-income space. If I could provide higher quality low-income, affordable housing, I believed there would be an overwhelming response—and I was right. Having owned over twenty-two mobile home parks in more than eleven states, I have yet to have a significant issue with demand. Our model allows us to derive substantial profits while dignifying the low-income housing experience.

Prior to starting my mobile home park business, I had to clearly identify what my goals were for investing in real estate. Some questions that you might want to ask yourself are:

- What is your monthly income goal?

- What is your long-term equity goal? How long is long-term for you?

- Are you looking for a one-time lump sum or residual? (If you are like me, the answer is both!)

As I began my business fresh out of college, my initial goal was $10,000 per month of net income. This answered the dollar-amount question, and it also answered the type of income that I was looking for: residual with long-term equity. Residual income is sometimes called "mailbox money," which is the money that comes in on a recurring, and sometimes passive, basis. Passive residual income is the holy grail for most Americans, even though most do not have the competency to create it. Throughout this book, I will continue to outline ways that you can create this type of income for you and your family.

For example, imagine not having to go to work for the next two months and having enough passive, residual income to maintain your current lifestyle. That's what passive income looks like if you choose to embrace it. If an investor purchases a mobile home park—and buys it correctly—it can net $2,000 to $30,000 a month in residual income, depending on the size and location of the property. And who is to say that you can only have one?

I wish that I could have the opportunity to take you with me and show you what I do every day to build and maintain our mobile home park business. Mentorship has been repeatedly identified as one of the best ways to gain applied knowledge in a field of study. While it would be an honor (and fun!) to work with you individually, I realize that it may not be realistic. This book is my way of making the knowledge available for application for those of you who are willing to take the initiative to take what's available on these pages and put it into action in your own life. I am looking forward to sharing with you how to build a real-estate business from the ground up, covering the ins and outs of finding and identifying property, negotiating and contracting, due diligence, financing, and management. It is your job to strap in, take notes, and gain understanding so that you can jump on a good deal when it is in front of you. And there will be many good deals that cross your path. The question is, will you be competent enough to recognize them?

Overlooked Market

For many investors and everyday people alike, the thought of owning a mobile home park would be right next to owning a septic cleaning business or earthworm farm. This market is not at the top of most investors' lists. In fact, it's not even on their radar. That is one thing that attracted me to this market. In addition to the mobile home park business being somewhat obscure, I loved the fact that I was able to serve the low-income segment of our population with quality housing. I look at my business today and smile to myself because it is more relevant today than it was when I first began, and I believe the future will only be brighter for reasons we will discuss in future chapters.

When it comes to mobile home parks, when making an offer, you will rarely find a bidding war going on. Bidding wars are a bit of an oxymoron in the current economy, but the point is that there are few skilled players in the mobile home park space, which allows for incredible opportunity for you and me. The limited legitimate competition in the niche market of investing in mobile home parks provides time and clear minds to come to a positive agreement on price and terms that work to a mutual benefit.

Why Do Mobile Home Parks Make Sense Financially?

When you spend as much time as I have performing cash-flow analysis on different areas of real estate, you begin to notice specific areas of opportunity. Right off the bat, mobile home parks appealed to me compared to other types of real estate for a number of reasons:

1. They provide typically higher cash-on-cash returns.

2. They carry typically higher capitalization rates.

3. They have a lower cost per door ($10,000 compared to $50,000+ for an apartment complex with similar rent structure).

4. Due to economics and other reasons, seller financing is more prevalent.

Today, the economics of a mobile home park transaction are as compelling as they ever have been. Due to the housing boom and then bust, the demand for quality low-income, affordable housing is on the rise with no end in sight. This trend directly benefits the mobile home park industry, as no other asset class can provide a quality living experience for such a low cost in today's market.

As is often quoted, "The poor will always be with you." This biblical reference has been true and remains true today. As you can imagine, this is a positive fact for the future of mobile home park demand. That means you have a built-in market for the future and an opportunity to serve the poor and make their living conditions safe, clean, and functional while running a profitable business.

Morally Positive

As a provider of low-income housing for the lower income or working poor, I sleep well at night. I've made an unbelievable living, but I also have a sense of personal fulfillment. I know that I'm helping thousands of others to sleep in a place that is safe, clean, and functional. It's rewarding and mutually beneficial for everyone.

In addition to running a profitable business that serves the lower income market, we also look for opportunities to provide additional perks for our customer base. A recent example of this was a partnership we developed with a nonprofit organization. This particular organization focuses on serving underprivileged children by creating an educational day in the community where they live. We certainly share their passion and partnered with them to hold educational days in our parks. Not all the families have computers in their homes, so this nonprofit organization brings in computers, materials, and equipment and provides the kids with an educational experience. They teach children basic computers, problem-solving, and interpersonal, practical living skills. The nonprofit was fulfilled by serving the children they desire to reach, the tenants and children were positively impacted by this experience, and we were honored to share in the service of our community.

Although the number-one goal in our business is to be profitable, we enjoy identifying areas in our business where we can give back to the communities we own and operate. Running our business in this way has provided for a tremendous sense of personal fulfillment.

A Largely Unsophisticated Market

Over the years of investing in multifamily residential and specializing in mobile home parks, we have built systems upon systems that allow us to enter a transaction knowing what our outcome will be. We have developed many systems, from acquisitions to billing our tenants for utilities and everything in between. In order to help you get up and running more quickly than I did, I have provided you with a number of these resources on the Trailer Cash website (www.trailercash.com).

For the most part, the mobile home park industry is largely unsophisticated and is saturated with moms and pops whose idea of rent rolls would be the back of an envelope thrown on their dashboard. With the document library and systems that we have built to streamline our business, you surely stand to benefit from the information provided in this book and on www.TrailerCash.com.

Many times upon acquiring a property, we find the business is so unrefined that we can improve profits by making a few simple changes to operations while simultaneously improving the experience for the tenants within the first few months of ownership. As an example, we purchased a mobile home park in Kentucky a few years back. During our due diligence, we found some irregularities in the seller's income. After some easy analysis, we found the manager with her hands in the till. She was taking approximately $1,500 per month. After some additional investigation, we found out that the manager had been stealing $1,500 per month for the last several years and the owner knew it. As the $1,500 per month was not reflected in the seller's income statement, we proceeded to close on that park, fire the manager, and in doing so saw a $1,500 bump in our net profit in the first month. That represents an extra $18,000 a year—not bad at all! This opportunity was simple to identify through our systematic approach to due diligence, as well as operations.

Misconceptions about Investing in Mobile Home Parks (MHPs)

There are a multitude of misconceptions our society has about mobile home parks and this type of investing. I could easily come up with one misconception for every chapter of this book. Misconceptions are like myths generated by stubborn ignorance and lack of willingness to dig deeper for the facts. Of course, these misconceptions create a wide-open market for us!

The biggest misconception is that a lot of investors believe a trailer park is synonymous with what some folks call "trailer trash." They picture old guys with shotguns running you off their properties, police appearances through the night, and gnarly, bearded bikers who drink beer with breakfast. These are just some of the classic stereotypes perpetuated in film and TV. When you visit enough mobile home parks, you will understand why people say there may be a little truth to every stereotype. However, the mistaken idea that mobile home parks are synonymous with "trailer trash" is a component in making this niche market a treasure trove of opportunities. So be very glad for the misperception. If investors were *not* sitting in judgment of these types of communities, this particular market would oversaturate with demand very quickly.

In short, the reality is that others' misperceptions create great opportunities for you. The people who live in mobile home parks are part of our human family. Each one is valuable, and the large percentage of them will earn your respect as trustworthy, rent-paying tenants.

> The people who live in mobile home parks are part of our human family. Each one is valuable.

So Why Aren't More Investors Buying MHPs?

Here is a question I get a lot: *If mobile home parks are so great, why aren't more investors buying them?*

Great question! The answer is so simple that you almost can't appreciate it. The comment I get the most when people find out what type of opportunity investing in mobile home parks really is goes something like this: "I had no idea something that ugly was actually making any money." Most people look at the general stereotype of a mobile home park and don't even consider it an option for their investment portfolio. It is kind of nice to see how the herds of people move in a direction that leaves this niche market opportunity available for investors who are willing to look at the numbers and the business model for what it is—an opportunity.

Some investors assume that if mobile home park tenants are on a fixed income or earn a lower-income wage, that providing housing to this segment of the population couldn't possibly result in a profitable endeavor. However, we are not offering high-end homes to these folks. We are offering a housing solution that fits within their limited budget. The valuable point in this is that there are a lot more people living in our country today on a limited budget than those that can afford high-end housing options. If you were going to open a business, would you rather have a product that over half of the population has a demand for or try to compete for the business of a few? The answer to that question should be easy. It should also indicate why this investment niche makes sense.

> I find it ironic that most Americans work for the rich and wind up poor, while we serve the poor and have become wealthy. Which would you rather do?

I find it ironic that most Americans work for the rich and wind up poor, while we serve the poor and have become wealthy. Which would you rather do?

Why Mobile Home Parks?

As strange as it may sound, a mobile home park is an excellent place to start building your financial independence. Looking beyond the stigmas and stereotypes of trailer parks, we discovered several advantages and few disadvantages, if any, to investing in what we like to call "trailer cash."

We provide affordable housing for a growing population of folks who are in some cases only a few paychecks away from being homeless. Oftentimes we are buying these parks from owners who did not take very good care of the property and did not maximize its profitability. Some owners actually let the quality of the property get so far degraded that it lowers the value, creating an opportunity for a great value buy on your end. Many times there are a few systematic changes which can be done quickly that will increase the value of the property for the investor as well as the quality of the experience for the consumer. We are in the business of upgrading the parks so they can operate in a way that maximizes income, minimizes expenses, and raises the overall value for everyone.

Although I get the stigmas that come with mobile home parks, I wonder why obnoxious drunken behavior is always associated with a certain class of people. In the end, the poor do not own a monopoly on poor behavior. The way I see it, there is no difference between someone sitting on the front porch of a mobile home after work with a Budweiser and a bunch of twenty-somethings hanging outside a bar drinking martinis. Of course, the martini drinkers are the ones putting their bar tabs on their credit cards, so they can at least give the appearance of being upper class.

People become overextended in every economic class. The only difference is the number of zeros at the end of their paychecks. Even movie stars such as Brad Pitt, Reese Witherspoon, and Denzel Washington live in trailers on location when shooting films. And I have met plenty of mobile home park residents who have downsized, retired, and do not live there as a last resort. However, the obvious reality is that many live there because that is their only option, and I am glad to help.

The majority of tenants in mobile home parks are good, hard-working, blue-collar people. At the end of the day, I am not judging anyone lest I be judged; I am evaluating an investment strategy. A big mistake many people make is to think themselves better than someone else. I am not better than my tenants and have learned a host of valuable lessons from many of those to whom I provide housing.

Yes, I've seen tenants missing a few teeth and kids running around with the wrong shoes on their feet, but everyone needs a place to live. I've met some mobile home park residents who work harder than anyone I know, and I have met plenty of rich folks who have never worked a day in their lives.

A specific example of an experience with one of our tenants was with a woman who lived in one of our parks and helped us out sometimes when we needed it. She was a woman whose greatest pride was in her daughter making straight As at the local high school. But they were caught on the hamster wheel of life because, like most parents, they wanted more for their kids than they ever had. On one of my visits to the park to check on operations, I encouraged her daughter to apply for colleges and talked to her about how to write college application essays. I had been in the same spot at her age, and my English teacher had helped me. The following year, this girl became the first one in her family to go on to college. I take zero credit for that. I just want to make the point: access to information, application, and perseverance is often the only difference between staying stuck or moving forward.

Chapter 3

How Do I Find the Deals?

After an investor realizes how much opportunity there is in the mobile home park business, they typically ask me, "How do I find the deals?"

Great profit-generating deals are not usually found; they are created. Like we have discussed, low-income, affordable housing is in great demand and creating quite the buzz as the word gets out about the opportunity with mobile home parks. Within the segment of "affordable housing" or "low-income housing," there are multiple options available: single-family homes, townhomes, condos, apartment buildings, and mobile home parks. Of all those options I just listed, most investors are least interested in mobile home parks due to the many misperceptions mentioned in chapter 2. And that's good for you because you'll have less competition in the mobile home park business.

My First Deal

Probably the best way to help you find your first deal is to tell you how I found mine. I told you that I had lived in an unfinished garage apartment to save money while I attended the University of Central Florida. My plan was to graduate with a BA in business and a BS in psychology, but I wondered, *Where's that going to get me?* My greatest educational experience seemed to be going on where I worked—at the leasing office of an off-campus apartment complex.

Originally when I graduated with my undergraduate degrees, my plan was to go on to law school as an advanced form of business school. The other obvious alternative after graduation was to go into traditional corporate America. From an internship that I had while in college for a major company in the Central Florida area, I learned how the corporate world worked and what it represented:

- Most people in the corporate world hated their jobs.

- The politics were incessant.

- In order to move up, you waited on someone to die, retire, or be fired.

This was not attractive to me as a young, ambitious college graduate. I was very confident in my work ethic and ability to contribute to someone else's business, but I was aware that working for someone else wouldn't leave me much to show for all of my hard work and time. Like most people, I don't mind working hard if I know I'll be correspondingly rewarded for that effort.

Most people start their careers seeing the corporate environment as security, but I have spoken with thousands of people that will tell you it's a trap. The perceived security eats years off their lives while they never really get the opportunity to build something for themselves. I was not afraid of the work. I was concerned about the house of cards I would build if I chose the traditional path.

> The rent checks that came in every month for my employer were the reality check I needed to make a move.

At that point in my life, I knew the only way I could achieve financial freedom and independence was by owning my own business. Our country is built on the entrepreneurial spirit, and this is one of the things that makes me so proud to be an American. We are in this great country because our founders opted to travel an undefined road rather than take one that was paved for them with its false sense of security.

I worked and interned as a young adult, and I liked my bosses. I did not resent them for benefiting from my hard work, but it was clear to me who was creating wealth—and it wasn't me as the employee. I wanted to be on the other side of the table. The rent checks that came in every month for my employer were the reality check I needed to make a move.

I thought, *How do you go from tenant to landlord?*

As I saw the amount my roommates and I were paying in rent each month, a simple thought crossed my mind: *Why not me?* The only thing missing was a property. I knew I didn't really have any credit, and I didn't have any type of savings to work with, but I decided to start looking at property anyway. Everyone I talked to about this thought I was crazy and thought I had no business even considering buying a property at my age. Everyone looked at me as a college kid working several jobs to make my way through, and their perception was that I was out of my league. I learned quickly that sometimes you just shut your mouth and do what you have to do. In the end, I have learned that if a person cannot tell you what you should do in your life, they have no right to tell you what you can't do—this goes for everyone.

So that is what I did. I started to look for property in areas where I knew other students would be willing to live. I also started working on the math of making a mortgage payment, taxes, and insurance. But I needed the right property. Mobile home parks were not even on my radar at the time. So every day, I opened the local newspaper and looked under "Homes for Sale" in the classifieds. I began calling and working over the properties for sale that I had found.

All this time, I heard from friends and family, who said:

- You are nuts.
- What are you thinking?
- This can't work.

I kept right on calling anyway, knowing I could buy a house, but not knowing how.

Soon after, I called a condo listing while on my work break and spoke with an agent who told me the condo for sale was near campus. It was $105,000. I went to take a look at it right away. Even with my two paying jobs, I did not have enough savings for a down payment or closing costs. But I knew I could make the situation work if I could come up with the initial $7,000.

> I kept calling properties for sale, knowing I could buy a house, but not knowing how.

Seven thousand dollars was a tremendous amount of money for me at the time, so I knew that I either had to think or quit. After a few days of thinking about creative alternatives, I had an idea. If I applied for a student loan for about $7,000 and got it, that would be all I would need to close on the property. Shortly thereafter, I applied for the loan, got it, and I was in the game.

My real-estate education first began with whether or not to use an agent, and if so, what agent to pick. For reasons I will discuss later, real-estate agents do not always provide valuable assistance for the investment community. You will learn that I am not anti-agent, just pro-profit. But hindsight being 20/20, I found out what the saying means, "You get what you pay for."

How Do I Find the Deals?

My real-estate education was just beginning. I used a real-estate agent to close the deal, assuming she was on my side. I quickly learned that agents want to close quickly, sell for the highest price, and minimize any potential challenges that could delay or eliminate a closing. I had committed the classic no-no of investing: I bought from an agent who had never even bought property herself.

I felt such a sense of accomplishment. I now owned a two-bedroom, two-bathroom condo near the university. The neighborhood where I purchased was filled with people that made more money than I did, yet despite this I had diligence, creativity, and perseverance on my side.

> I had committed the classic no-no of investing: I bought from an agent who had never even bought property herself.

Now that I was a homeowner, I immediately sought to be a landlord in order to derive enough revenue to cover my mortgage and other expenses. Thus I made my first mistake as a landlord: *do not rent to friends (or family)!* I had convinced a friend to move in with me and charged her fair-market value for the rent. Her rent almost met the mortgage payment, so my own rent actually went down. If you can believe it, I actually paid less to own my own property than I was paying to rent that awful room in the garage! I was also benefiting from the tax write-off of the interest while building equity. It was quite the deal.

After finding and negotiating a property for a good price, verifying demand, and closing on the property through creative financing strategies, the process now transitioned to operations (in other words, management). A few quick lessons I learned immediately in this next phase were: don't rent to friends, and get everything in writing.

My first mistake in the landlording experience was renting to a friend. Due to my friendship with my first tenant, I did not require a lease to be signed. At first everything was fine, but after a few months my tenant (friend) stopped paying rent. I quickly understood that just because I was going to honor my word, that did not mean the other person is going to honor theirs. Lesson: get everything in writing! Although it was a frustrating experience at the time that cost me several thousand dollars, this lesson has saved me literally hundreds of thousands over the years.

If you are wondering how you can go from being a renter to an investor, you can see how a college kid with hardly any cash or credit made the jump. While not a smooth transition, I got off the sidelines and into the game by taking a big step forward, and that was the first step toward building my business. This is a game, and before you play, you must know the rules.

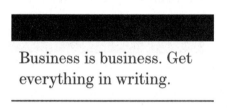

Business is business. Get everything in writing.

Now that I owned one property, combined with my experience in multifamily property management, my focus turned to multi-family ownership. While single-family residential investing can provide a good rate of return, I knew that it would be a much slower path to the destination that I had set my sights on. To meet my financial goals, I just needed to add a few zeros behind the number of units that I owned. I knew that what I had dreamed of was possible; I just needed to start moving in that direction.

I don't like to see when others give up on their dreams only because they don't see the way or they don't know the *how*. Never lay down your dream and opt for the predictable. Do you want to be predictably mediocre or dare for greatness with a possibility of failure, realizing that to fail simply means to try again? Like I said in the first chapter, you weren't born knowing how to breathe— you got spanked and learned on the job.

I knew it would work out, even before I knew *how* it would work out. Thank God I had the courage to act on that very first opportunity, in spite of everyone's warnings. Although everything with my first real-estate transaction did not go perfectly, it was a success built on action. That first deal immediately opened up so many more new opportunities for my future. Now I had established credit and built equity.

Digging for the Gold

Most treasure isn't found by tripping over it. If you want to find a mobile home park treasure, you'll need to locate an area that shows promise, get out your shovel, and dig through a pile of information until you see a glimmer of gold shine through. That's the exciting moment. But you have to be able to tell the difference between junk and treasure. Since I can't go with you personally, I have sorted through most of the preliminary junk for you. I'm practically giving you a treasure map here that will lead you to an investment that could change your and your family's life.

Here are the types of mobile home parks available:

- Family parks
- Senior communities (55 and older)
- Recreational vehicle parks (otherwise known as RV parks)

Each type of mobile home park has its own set of unique circumstances. If you're just starting out in this business, I recommend family parks. In fact, family mobile home parks are and have been our main area of investment.

Family parks

Family parks are the most common type of mobile home park, comprising over 90 percent of all parks in the market. They are also the easiest to occupy because they accept the broadest range of tenants and therefore are in the highest demand.

Let's quickly dispel a myth: mobile homes are mobile. The truth is, mobile homes are not really all that mobile. It costs about $2,000–3,000 for a single-wide and about $6,000 for a double-wide to move to a new location outside the park. Due to that expense, tenants of mobile homes are much more likely to keep their home in your park, especially if you treat them with the respect they deserve.

Senior communities

Parks designated for tenants fifty-five and over were legalized under the Fair Housing Amendment Act of 1988. On the plus side, these types of mobile home parks have lower turnover, as the tenants are often retirees who, once they have moved in and settled down, tend to stay put. They are not like the younger generation that may have to follow a job out of the area. While we love the idea that senior mobile home parks represent a long-term consumer/tenant base, older tenants present different challenges.

> Tenants of mobile homes are much more likely to keep their home in your park, especially if you treat them with the respect they deserve.

A particular challenge with these types of mobile home parks is that it is harder to raise rent because the residents are often on a fixed income. Even though an increasing number of baby boomers are reaching this age group, the 55-and-over crowd still represents a smaller portion of the general population and therefore shrinks the tenant pool you can draw from. (Conversely, family parks welcome people of all ages, including senior citizens. No one is left out.)

In the event that a senior tenant does move, there is a longer expected period of vacancy in most cases, due to the restricted tenant base. If a mobile home lot goes unoccupied for a bit longer in a senior park, the owner of that mobile home park will experience a loss in income, which detracts from your overall profitability. And it is likely that a lot in a senior community will sit vacant longer due to the restrictions on who is allowed to move in.

A large segment of the senior community is retired, and their tenants spend a lot of time onsite. That could mean additional expenses like game rooms, pools, clubhouses, bingo nights, and so on to keep your property in high demand and competitive with other like properties. That's not necessarily a bad thing, but it is worth considering these types of potential expenses when you're deciding what type of property you wish to acquire. Some seniors might have so much time on their hands that they may take it upon themselves to come to the office and complain to the manager about items that may have not otherwise been an issue. This could be as simple as a new rock that is encroaching on the shuffleboard court. Maintenance costs can also be higher because, frankly, the tenants have the time to talk to each other and get everyone all worked up about basic things. Of course, we want all our tenants to be happy and safe in our parks. Just be prepared to listen (and sometimes laugh) if you are going to target this specific type of mobile home park.

RV parks

We avoid RV parks. Period. Some people out there make money with them, but some people make money selling a half-eaten Snickers that they fished out of a garbage can. Simply put, these parks are more hassle than they're worth for the bulk of investors. RV parks are difficult to occupy, require higher investment for amenities and activities, have a high turnover (churn), require more costly advertising, and much more. The tenants tend to be harder to manage because of their often transient lifestyle. An RV park requires persistent advertising due to the high turnover, as well as higher security and crime challenges. If that doesn't discourage you, think about this—RVs are "roll-ready," which means people can disappear pretty quickly when the rent comes due.

One of the major challenges in purchasing an RV park is that lenders do not want to touch them, due to the seasonal, inconsistent income. Besides, RV parks require a lot of management, and my husband and I decided early on that we want to be married to each other, not our investments.

What You Need to Proceed

There are a few things you need to know about when prospecting and evaluating a property. The sample of the Mobile Home Park Quick Evaluation Sheet on page 33 will help you begin your phone conversation with the potential seller. Not only will it serve you to be organized, concise, and purposeful in your property prospecting, but also your thorough approach has a valuable impact on the potential seller's perception of you. Whoever you are talking to will know you are serious about buying the park and running it well. Think of it as playing detective, sniffing out deals and hunting down clues. Have fun with it. Every detail is a clue that will count for or against the investment's viability.

Play detective, sniffing out deals and hunting down clues.

For a complete version of the Mobile Home Park Quick Evaluation sheet, please visit www.trailercash.com.

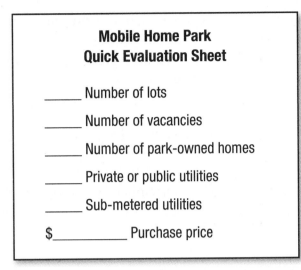

Don't be too quick to write off a park as a potential profit-maker by saying, "A four-thousand-dollar utility bill? No thanks." We check that off on our list as a positive. Why? Because if there are financial and management inefficiencies sucking profits right out of the owner's pockets, that same amount will get added to your profit column as soon as you make the transition to individual meters.

Understanding the difference between a problem and an opportunity is the specific reason you will be able to put deals together while other investors continue to say that they are looking for a good deal but haven't found one yet. As I always say, good deals are often created, not found. What others see as a liability, you will sometimes see as an opportunity. And when you see what looks like a good opportunity, then, "Run, Forest, run!"

The good news is that there's always a demand for low-income housing. In order to make the highest return, you want to invest where the demand is the highest. Don't limit yourself if you don't have to. Family parks are open to the masses. The other types of parks narrow your pool of applicants and lessen your income potential while possibly maximizing your expenses. Contrary to popular belief, tenant-owned homes in a family park is the best-case scenario for a mobile home park investor. Making profitable investments will give you the time to expand your current investment portfolio.

Focusing on the purpose for this chapter, let's ask how to find the deals. Where do you look?

The Search Begins

The process of looking for a mobile home park can be extremely interesting and definitely entertaining. You can learn information about mobile home park availability, pricing, and value through several different methods:

- Brokers
- Mailings
- In-person visits
- Online
- Other resources
- Cold calls

Brokers

Brokers are not necessarily our first method of choice, but if you would like to begin with utilizing a broker for your mobile home park search, you can find them through web searches, Multiple Listing Service (MLS) listings, the Chamber of Commerce, and websites that are specific to this type of investment.

If you decide to use a broker, be sure to have as much information on your financing situation as you can prior to your conversation with the broker. As financing is a significant challenge in an economically contracted cycle, a broker will not give you the time of day if you start stuttering when they talk to you about how you are planning to finance the property. You must position yourself as a knowledgeable buyer from financing to due diligence to management and so on. It's been said, "Fake it 'til you make it." Keep that phrase in mind as you begin to build your business. No one will believe in you if you don't. This book will give you the resources to have a professional conversation with an industry insider.

As in any business deal, be nice! A friendly personality will go a long way. As you build a relationship with your broker through mobile home park closings, you will find that your broker is more willing to burn the midnight oil on your behalf—finding deals, providing pocket listings, leveraging their relationships for your benefit, and so on. In the end, your performance speaks, or as is more commonly said, money talks. And there is nothing wrong with being rewarded for your efforts.

Having said that, do *not* assume your broker is your friend. The broker is a businessman or businesswoman, just like you. The seller and the broker get paid at closing, so they are clearly motivated by a closing taking place. It has been found that an individual with a license will allow their home to sit on the market longer, waiting for top dollar, than a similar type of home for a client. The point is the broker will act in their best interest. Buyers get paid after closing, and buyers make their money by buying right. We'll talk about due diligence in a later chapter. For now, just realize that your broker should not and will not do your due diligence for you.

Mailings

Perhaps you feel more comfortable beginning your search by sending out mailings to potential sellers. You may mail postcards, letters, or e-mails. Here's a sample letter:

> *Dear Owner,*
> *I am interested in purchasing a mobile home park in your area. If you have thought about selling your mobile home park or would be interested in selling, please give us a call. We will go through the information on your park with you quickly and will work to create a deal that will work for both parties.*

Be sure to provide your phone number, fax number, and e-mail address. You want to make it as easy as possible for a seller to get in touch with you.

In-person visits

Some people find visiting in person the only way to do business. Others find it frightening and would rather e-mail or call. We choose to do the latter, as doing an in-person visit on every prospective property would be far too time consuming to be effective.

The positive aspect of visiting in person is that you gather most of the information about your prospective property yourself. Also, you get to know the manager and/or owner much more easily through a personal visit rather than a phone call. You will learn in future chapters when it is recommended to do an onsite property visit. In short, feeling the absolute need to visit a property before putting it under contract is an indication that you do not know what you are doing.

Online

- www.loopnet.com
- www.mobilehomeparkstore.com
- www.mhvillage.com
- www.mhpinfo.com
- www.bizbuysell.com
- www.craigslist.com
- www.ebay.com
- www.switchboard.com
- www.yellowpages.com

Search for more at www.google.com

Other resources

- Newspapers (or find local papers online)
- Mobile homes for sale in the classifieds
- City hall
- The tax assessor's office
- Other park owners

Cold calls

The best property to buy is the property not yet for sale. Cold calling is the best way to gain access to these properties, and it is what our business is built on. Many times I am asked by newbie investors, "You mean, you actually just call people out of the blue?" To which I reply, "Yep." Crazy, isn't it? It's like brushing your teeth: it makes sense, but not everybody does it.

You can get the best and most valuable information by speaking directly with the owner, and sometimes the manager. Just like in any sales process, you need to make sure that you are speaking with the individual who understands the circumstances and is the decision-maker. The owner is always going to have the final say, but sometimes the manager knows the property better than the actual owner. The information-gathering process can be collaborative; however, the owner is primarily the person that you need to speak with. They will be the person(s) that you will be putting the deal together with. Gather as much information as you can over the phone, as it will:

- Reduce risks

- Save travel expenses

- Increase profits later when negotiating

- Uncover unseen opportunities

- Let the owners know you are serious

- Provide access to information on local park competition as you talk with other potential parks

It's true. The most successful salespeople in the world excel at cold calling. Yet cold calling may be one of the most irrational fears out there. Most of the time, the person on the other end of the phone is friendly and happy enough to tell you anything you want to know. Our very first mobile home park deal is a perfect example how simple cold calling can be.

As I mentioned before, cold calling has been the most profitable for me. Here are a few tips to help you navigate that first call:

- Most owners like to deal with an individual.

- Be smart with property managers. (They are your allies.)

- Take good notes. (You'll need them later.)

- Jot down park information, timeline for communication, and personal information.

- Speak with the owner.

- Practice what you are going to say before you call.

- Be friendly.

- Give the impression that you are a knowledgeable buyer.

- Get any extra info they are willing to provide (just had a water main break, etc.).

How Do I Find the Deals?

Being friendly should go without saying, but people forget there is a real person on the other end of the phone. They will most likely be caught off guard by the call, so make friendly conversation. Introduce yourself and describe the purpose of your call briefly and slowly. These cold calls are very exciting, as the person on the other end of the phone line could be the owner of the mobile home park that will set you on your way to financial freedom!

As a woman in the world of real estate, I have found many advantages to being a female in this business. And I will just say this right off the bat: I am not a man-hater. However, the predominance of men in the real-estate business is undeniable, and it is considered by some women to be more of a man's world. I have met many women who view this as a disadvantage, and I think that this perspective is hocus pocus. Men and women are different, no question about it, but when it comes to running your real-estate-investment business, there is no reason a female cannot perform at the same level as her male counterpart.

I actually think that as a woman, we have an advantage with dealing with the sellers. Men like talking to women, and women like talking with women. In my experience, as it relates to cold calling, a woman has a competitive advantage in terms of prospecting. The ladies we have hired have proven more effective than the guys on the cold calls. There are several examples of this, but here is one. Once, two of our researchers happened to call the same mobile home park owner in the same week. The seller quoted two different prices: $50,000 more for the guy. Maybe the seller suddenly got ambitious, or maybe guys have their guard up around other guys. We think it was because our female caller was more pleasant and perhaps more disarming. This, paired with all of the successful mobile home park closings that have been initiated by some of the women that work on our team, demonstrate that any woman wanting to build a mobile home park business has nothing to worry about.

Sounding like a knowledgeable buyer will come naturally as you become a more seasoned investor. In the meantime, you will learn as you go, and that's okay. If you are nervous, practice, practice, practice! The most important thing is that you start. It's important to act.

> The most important thing is that you start. It's important to act.

The point here is that the person on the other end may assume that you are a solicitor only there to waste his or her time, so it's key that you find a way to personally connect and let them know it is your desire to buy from them—not the other way around. Let them know your name and that you are interested in purchasing their mobile home park. Ask them if you could have a few minutes of their time to answer some questions about their park. If not, ask if you can schedule some time to call back later. Stay friendly and professional, even if they tell you they are not interested in selling. I always leave my contact information with the seller for a possible purchase in the future. Before we hang up, I express my curiosity about under what conditions they *would* be interested in selling. We have had park owners call us back later because the call got them curious about the benefits of selling. We always send a follow-up letter to every person we talk to about purchasing their property and leave the door open for a potential investment opportunity at a later time.

The Phone Is Your Metal Detector and Your Best Friend

Once I realized what an attractive investment mobile home parks were, I proceeded to pursue this area of investment in the same way I did to acquire the off-campus apartment—I started making calls.

It may sound tedious, but doing your own legwork to identify a property to purchase provides a market advantage because there are excellent deals that have never been listed in the yellow pages or even the MLS. While others were checking the MLS listings or surfing the web, I picked up the phone and started beating the pavement to contact all the mobile home parks I could find in the markets we were interested investing in.

Think of it this way. If you knew someone in your neighborhood had a million dollars in his house and wanted to get rid of it, wouldn't you be willing to knock on a few doors to find it? Of course you would. But so many people we meet are unwilling to pick up a phone and ask a perfect stranger if he is interested in selling his property. People want some-

News flash: if you don't step outside the norm, normal will be your lifelong neighbor.

thing extraordinary from their lives but many times are unwilling to doing anything outside the ordinary to make that happen. News flash: if you don't step outside the norm, normal will be your lifelong neighbor. This book's purpose is to get you to reach higher, try harder, and go outside what is currently the norm for you. Many people do not want to do cold calling because it sounds like a lot of work. Let's just be clear: if you don't want to work, this isn't the business for you. While I am blessed to have the ability to choose to work, it is work nonetheless.

As I have found many people are intimidated by the cold calling process, I have come up with a list of possible responses so that you know what to expect:

1. No, I haven't thought about selling, and no, I'm not interested.

2. No, I haven't thought about selling, but yes, I would be interested.

3. Yes, I've thought about it but haven't gotten around to it.

4. Yes, I've thought about it, and yes, I am interested.

On extremely rare occasions, you might encounter a jerk who yells at you and hangs up because they think you're a telemarketer (or the IRS). Believe it or not, a gentleman literally thought I was an IRS auditor looking into his "other set of books." But the majority of the people that you speak with will be friendly, and some will be ready to sell—and one is all you need. One properly performing mobile home park could replace the average American's annual salary.

In the next chapter, I'll share various avenues you can use to find property. The first step is to get a good picture of exactly what you're looking for in a mobile home park investment. Read on!

Chapter 4

Criteria for Mobile Home Park Locations

As a successful mobile home park owner, you'll want to be strategic and savvy. This means setting your emotions aside! And that's because the best location for your new investment might not be where you want it to be. The best location will be in a highly populated area with a vast array of jobs for blue-collar workers and resasonable land cost to acquire. So if you live in Beverly Hills and want a mobile home park down the block, chances are that location may not be right due to land value and cost acquisition. There are great parks in very nice neighborhoods, but make sure your decision is based on all the things I will talk about here while selecting your desired location. As with any business decision, make a decision based on the business of it—the numbers. Don't make a decision solely based on convenience to you!

Obviously people do business all over the country, but there are certain indicators of ideal market conditions to look for and other factors to avoid. These are our main criteria for deciding in which area to invest:

1. Accessibility

2. Market stability and growth (new jobs in the area, diversity, etc.)

3. Population stability and growth (ie., demand)

4. Demographics

5. Low land value compared to market rents

6. Is there a Wal-mart nearby? Fast-food restaurants? (Wal-mart and other major anchors are a plus.)

7. Low property taxes

8. Business-friendly laws that govern the area

9. Big-city or small-town advantages

Believe it or not, there is a pretty big swath of the country that meets these criteria. Not all variables will line up in your favor, so you have to weigh out the good, the bad, and the ugly. For example, when it came to possibly investing in Texas, we found that property taxes there are relatively high. Yet people like to live there because there is no state income tax. While the property taxes are high, the cost of land is still pretty low. In addition to the low land cost, the rate of growth in population makes it attractive. Texas is also a very business-friendly state. We followed the numbers and now own in over eleven states, and growing—one of which is Texas, where we now own several parks. You will have to weigh all these factors according to your own long-term plan. Let's go through each.

Accessibility

As I always say, fish where the fish are. You can drop your line in the desert, and one day you may get water—but the question is, how long do you want to wait? At the end of the day, you will be better off looking into markets that support profitability and investing, rather than seeking to force an investment in your hometown, simply based on proximity.

What it comes down to is your ability to manage a property. You will either be a good manager or a bad manager—proximity does not play a role. It's tempting to start in your own backyard because it seems more convenient. If you are waiting to invest in something near your house, you could be waiting for a long time. I met a gentleman who told me he has wanted to purchase a mobile home park for the last thirty years, but he just never came across a good deal. I asked him where he was looking. He answered, "My hometown." I wouldn't spend thirty years or three years waiting on a hometown investment. Besides, if you are too close to your properties, they can potentially dominate your life, and not in a positive way. By not having all of our investments in our hometown, we don't have to deal with the minutiae of day-to-day management and can focus our energy every day on growing the business with more bargain hunting.

We have found it is best to look at mobile home park investments like grandchildren: enjoy your time with them, but let someone else take care of them day to day. You must treat your mobile home park investments like a business. If you treat your business like a business, you will make business money. If you treat your business like a hobby, you will make hobby money—which is oftentimes zero.

> If you treat your business like a business, you will make business money. If you treat your business like a hobby, you will make hobby money.

Many people believe that a business closer to home will be easier to manage, but to achieve scale in mobile home parks, you want to manage your business through systems and delegate the everyday responsibilities to onsite managers. Let me demonstrate. Do you believe that you make a better hamburger than McDonald's does? You are probably nodding your head yes. How much money would you make a year selling your hamburgers? How much income does McDonald's produce each year selling their hamburgers? The point of this is that you may make the best hamburger on earth, but if you do not have the proper system for operations in place, your business cannot perform to the fullest of its ability. It will not matter if your business is across the street or across the country, the key is to have a system for operations in place.

As an active investor, you will find it impossible to grow correctly while trying to be the onsite manager. You will spend all your time managing and paying yourself how much per hour? Instead, you need to take your higher-level skill set and find more deals.

Stability or high growth

Ideally, it would be nice to find an area with rising property values and job growth, but boomtowns can also go bust. Stable towns are better than boom-and-bust towns. We like stable, which means a consistent and somewhat predictable economy.

If you were to type "Houston, Texas" into www.bestplaces. net, you would see the same statistics we did—a strong population growth of 9.77 percent between 2000 and 2009. While those numbers may have presented challenges for urban planners there, that same information should jump off the page and sing to you, "Great cash flow!" There is a powerful indicator right off the bat telling you that people are moving from all directions into Texas.

Any area that is growing enough to offer diverse employment opportunities also creates special investment opportunities. If you buy a mobile home park on the outskirts of Houston today, for example, you know where it will be in ten years? Right in the middle of a river of commerce. Not a stream or a trickle, but a river of economic flow and a swelling number of people looking for someplace to live in a hurry, potentially competing for the lots in your park. If you decided to buy a park there, this would also indicate that your land value would eventually greatly exceed what it was when you bought it, and sooner rather than later. But historical growth is no guarantee of future growth, so you need a well-rounded picture of the market.

Many tenants of mobile home parks are blue-collar workers, so look for a diverse spectrum of employers with a fair amount of manufacturing or industrial jobs. Again, we're offering low-income, affordable housing.

We have all heard "location, location, location." When someone hears that phrase, they picture a beautiful high-rise in Miami on South Beach. The term *location* speaks to land value, appreciation, highest and best use, and so on. With what we are talking about, location lends itself to quality of the market, as it will impact the financial performance of your invest-

Location can lend itself to jobs, per-capita income, and long-term growth prospects.

ment. Just because a property is on South Beach—which would be a great location—doesn't mean it will lead to cash flow. So when we discuss location, in terms of this discussion, location can lend itself to jobs, per-capita income, and long-term growth prospects.

Contact employers in town and city planners to learn their expectations for growth or if they're cutting back. Employer diversity, for example, reduces your risk of sudden vacancies. Be thorough in your inquiries of the area.

With www.bestplaces.net, you can drill down deeper and learn more details about different parts of Houston or any other town in the country by typing in specific zip codes. You can see the cost of living, the median home price, unemployment rates, and more. This is general information that will tell you when you're in the ballpark. You will ascertain more specifics later, once you've zoomed in on your preferred states and areas within those states.

Low land value

Currently, we are not focused on California, New York, Florida, or other places like parts of Nevada where the real-estate markets have traditionally been expensive and volatile. The high land values there make it very difficult to get a significant positive monthly income after all expenses are paid. For example, if I am buying a mobile home park for the purposes of the cash flow from the mobile home park, I am not going to pay the "highest and best use" land price that the seller thinks it would sell for if I were developing a hotel. If I am buying a mobile home park, I am paying for a mobile home park.

Wal-mart—the gold nugget

If you really want to take advantage of millions of dollars of demographic research without any cost to you, go to Google and search "Wal-mart." Take a look at Wal-mart locations. Wal-mart is not going to go into a market that is unstable, so they have already done a lot of basic research for you. All the mobile home parks we own are within a few minutes of a Wal-mart. We didn't buy them just because they were near this major retail anchor, but all other aspects made sense after we reviewed our due-diligence list (I'll explain that list later on), and the market certainly qualified and just happened to have a Wal-mart nearby. That's where your prime demographic will be. A major discount store anchoring a shopping center is always a good sign for a prospective mobile home park owner.

Low property taxes and business-friendly states

Is your chosen state landlord-friendly when it comes to the laws? Ultimately, you're looking for an environment, and a lot of factors contribute to that. For example, we don't view California as a business-friendly environment. Besides the cost of setting up an entity, which is almost six times the cost of one in Florida, California's rent controls, property taxes, city taxes, county taxes, and state taxes all add up to more money, time, and effort to do what you could do in other favorable states for less cost and hassle. First-time buyers often forget to calculate all these additional costs, only to find at the end of the year that their actual profit was less than expected due to unforeseen expenses. New York not only has high taxes but also is especially litigious. Why go through that hassle? There are forty-nine other states from which to choose.

Meanwhile, Michigan's land value and property taxes are low, but their job market and overall market are in severe decline. In regards to any job market, you can't predict the future. You can, however, mitigate unknown factors by researching all current information available.

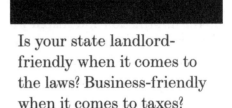

Is your state landlord-friendly when it comes to the laws? Business-friendly when it comes to taxes?

The good news is that there are plenty of good areas out there that won't keep you up at night, so there is no point getting into a market that's questionable.

Big cities vs. small towns

One more key factor to consider: the advantages and disadvantages of cities and towns. Larger cities offer certain advantages. Right off the bat, you've got more potential residents and more parks to choose from. It's easier to fly in and out of bigger cities, which is important because certain steps in the process definitely require in-person visits. We do not consider areas with fewer than 5,000 people because, just like any business, the more potential customers you have for your business, the better off you are going to be.

Mobile home parks perform best in communities with significant demand for low-income housing. It is optimal to find a park within commuter range of a large metropolitan statistical area (MSA). We like to look for developing areas on the outskirts of a growing city.

A Bit of Beginner's Luck

When I started in my pursuit of mobile home parks, I began by calling park owners in several different states. Quickly, I was able to identify some mobile home parks of interest. After one conversation with a seller of a park and gathering some basic information from him, I decided to call the city to verify some of the information provided to me. The woman that answered the phone pulled up the information and shared with me what I was looking for. It did not match up with what the local park owner had told me over the phone, and the differences killed the deal.

However, I had struck up a friendly conversation with this city employee. So when I expressed my disappointment, she asked if I might still be interested in another mobile home park in town, and I said, "Definitely." Her name was Judy, and she told me she knew a couple at her church who owned a mobile home park who wanted to sell it—and she herself happened to be a realtor who could broker the deal (this would be her first).

Judy had worked for the city for years and was very accommodating in helping me. The following Monday, she called me, as she had spoken to the potential sellers on Sunday at church. They were still interested in selling, and we were certainly interested in buying if everything in the park checked out.

We do not waste money on travel up front while we are considering a mobile home park for purchase, so we did all of our negotiations over the phone and via fax. Within a few days, we had the property under contract for $240,000 with twenty units. While this was my first mobile home park, and one of my smallest to date, it still amazes me that a small, twenty-unit mobile home park sells for the same price as one or two single-family houses! Think about it: would you rather own one or two units, or twenty for the same price? The answer is simple, isn't it? That is an extremely attractive component of multifamily investing—there's a lot more bang for your buck. The property was financed with a combination of conventional loan and seller financing, and we landed our first mobile home park property investment. (I'll talk more about financing in another chapter.)

Now You Know

You don't need a whole lot of time to start looking for mobile home parks, just the courage to start and the questions to ask. You don't have to have a lot of money to get started. You will just need the understanding and creativity to structure good deals. We will continue to discuss this as we go through the different phases of investing.

So go ahead and get started. Once you get the potential seller on the line and confirm some specific pieces of information you've identified, then work these basic questions into the conversation while you're speaking to the interested seller in regard to pricing:

- Have you thought about a price?
- Do you have a recent appraisal?
- Do you know what the tax-assessed value is?

Here are some important strategies:

- Get the potential seller to throw out the first number—this is extremely important.

- Clear a time to call back and gather the additional information from the Mobile Home Park Quick Evaluation Sheet.

- Use your Quick Evaluation sheet from www.trailercash.com—it is an efficient way to gather the information you need to evaluate the deal.

- If the potential buyer is ready to talk now, engage them immediately in further conversation!

Chapter 5

Being a Value-Conscious Investor

As a child, my family inched its way toward a better life one fixer-upper at a time until we ended up living in a good neighborhood, which is where I lived until I graduated from high school. As a young girl, I understood the value of real estate, as I saw how it improved the financial position of my family. The school I attended had a healthy mix of the have's and the have-not's. Plenty of my schoolmates were wealthy and drove cars to school they were given for their birthdays or for Christmas. I could barely afford my school yearbook, let alone a car. My mom still transported me to volleyball games, and I caught rides to school, to practice, or wherever I had to go. I certainly did a lot of walking, but my mind was always running.

When I turned sixteen, someone from our church who understood our family's circumstances donated a car for me to drive so that I could get myself to work, school, and practice. I can't necessarily say that I was riding in style, but at least I wasn't walking or trying to catch a ride. I was the proud new owner of a mid-80s Chevrolet Celebrity with no A/C.

Although the appearance of the car was less than stellar, I thought it was incredibly generous for someone to provide a car to a complete stranger, and my gratitude left no room for complaints. I appreciated that car and the generosity that was shown to me. It has always been my goal to bless others as I have been so richly blessed.

Growing up, I always appreciated my mother's hard work and determination. I saw firsthand the tremendous effort and potential risk involved in rehabbing and flipping a house. Although years later I would jump headfirst into the real-estate market, I was determined to do it differently and do it better.

The Value of Education

Instead of accepting a definition of myself as a "have-not," I knew there were other options for me if I chose them. Our U.S. Constitution states that all people are created equal and each of us has the right to life, liberty, and the pursuit of happiness. While we don't need someone to tell us that money doesn't make you happy, it certainly provides a greater level of freedom that allows for the pursuit of happiness. If you don't believe that financial resources can alleviate some pressure, try paying your bills with an empty bank account.

When I was in college, I met a lot of kids who blew off classes or didn't study much for tests. It absolutely amazed me. They didn't value their education because they had no perspective of where they would be in their future without it. Having to pay my own way through college, I appreciated it in the moment. I also understood the impact it would have on my future, given experiences from my past. The pressure of balancing several jobs, two majors, and multiple school clubs and activities developed many valuable skills that translate into our business operations today.

When I completed my degrees, I was very proud to have accomplished that. However, something I find interesting is that although I have those two degrees, I have never once had to provide a copy of one of my diplomas to be able to operate any area of my business. I am not saying that formal education has no value—it certainly does. What I am saying is that just because you haven't reached the level of formal education you would like—maybe you don't have a college degree—there is still no excuse for you not to be able to achieve the level of financial success you desire.

When I speak with people from different backgrounds, some of them say they didn't finish high school or college and feel this lack of education disqualifies them from building a successful business. Not true! You can absolutely do anything you want. After all, education is the process of acquiring particular knowledge or skills. That just so happens to be what you are doing right now as you read this book. A degree is not required to start a multimillion-dollar business.

In fact, studies have shown that 20 percent of millionaires do not have college degrees. Bill Gates and Richard Branson are probably the most well-known billionaire dropouts. Jumping in and starting a business is the best education you can get in business, psychology, law, economics, finances, and management. We definitely learn by doing. If you are waiting on the perfect circumstances to start your business, you are backing up.

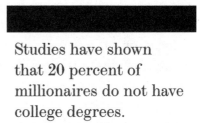

Studies have shown that 20 percent of millionaires do not have college degrees.

Lessons Learned

As I previously mentioned, my brothers and I were raised on a shoestring budget, and the most significant portion of our family's income came from buying land, building a home, and living there until it was sold or from simply rehabbing an existing structure. While this activity provided crucial income for my family (or equity for a greater home) and was appreciated, it was a feast-or-famine mentality. I always appreciated the value of a lump sum of cash but came to realize the greater importance of residual income quickly. After years of running a successful real-estate business, I value income first and equity second. After all, equity, in most cases, is for bragging rights at cocktail parties.

As I am a value investor, it is imperative to know how real estate is valued. When discussing value, I am not talking about the social value of a nice home but the method you use to determine an asset's intrinsic value. In real estate, there are three recognized methods for valuing an asset: the comparable sales method, the reproduction cost method, and the market rents method. You will need to pick the correct method of valuation depending on the type of asset you are interested in and your goals for it.

As previously mentioned, I desire income and equity and wish to focus on an asset, or assets, that produce both. Being that my greatest desire is monthly income, I want to use a model (or models) that places a value on income. The only model of the three that specifically values income is the market rents method, also known commonly as the income model.

I always find it ironic that most Americans purchase property using the comparable sales method when what they want, when asked, is income. The irony comes from the fact that the comparable sales method does not produce income. It's like trying to fit a square peg in a round hole.

It is important to know that the large majority of real-estate agents are trained only in the comparable sales method (although it is called comparative market analysis by many agents). Using an agent to find income-producing property to any significant degree is, in many cases, like trying to buy clothes from a naked person. In most cases, agents are not trained to invest or to ferret out income-generating properties. Many new investors immediately seek to rely on an agent when an agent's skill set isn't, for the most part, something that produces what we, as investors, are looking for: income.

Now that we have discussed the income model, our focus turns to the type of assets we would like to purchase. After many years of researching and purchasing assets, ranging from single-family residential properties to raw land and storage, I have found that mobile home parks produce more consistent net income, when properly acquired and managed, than any other property type of real estate that I have been involved in. They can not only provide income and equity, but are also relatively shielded from the changing economic cycles. As it says in Matthew 26:11, "The poor you will always have with you." If you do not believe the Bible as a valid reference, I would offer the following opinion and that is, "The poor have always been with us." As the economy passes between expansion and contraction, boom and bust, there are poor among us who need a quality place to live for a low cost. Based on current economic conditions, and looking to the future, I believe the need will only grow, and my business will correspondingly be in constant demand.

I feel it is important to mention that while my business is derived from serving low-income families with quality, affordable housing, I am not happy that there are poor among us. If I had the ability to wipe out poverty, I would, and I would identify other means to serve and make a profit. At the end of the day, poverty for many is a choice. There is always a way out if you are determined, willing to dream, and, most importantly, bold enough to take action in the face of those who would seek to discourage you.

I had a lady approach me years ago after an event where I spoke, and she said, "You know, I never chose to be poor." I, in turn, asked her if she had ever chosen to be wealthy, to which she replied no. It is important to mention that by not choosing, you made a choice. Not choosing to build a business and grow beyond your current circumstances to achieve your goals is a choice to not give your goals the opportunity to come to fruition. I also feel it is necessary to be clear in saying that money is never the goal; service of others is. Money is a byproduct of your passion for serving others and blessing their lives with a quality product.

Do the Numbers

We've talked about where to invest and how to find properties earlier in this book. That means you've looked at areas and evaluated markets. You have also started identifying particular properties in those markets. Now we can start evaluating your prospects. Real estate offers you the ability to create equity and income for yourself, if you are knowledgeable or in some cases lucky. If you do not wish to rely on luck, then you must run the numbers. The ability to perform a financial analysis on an investment is not only imperative but paramount to your success in this or any business. It is interesting to me that Americans spend more time researching their depreciating vehicle or the latest fashions than any investment they put their hard-earned money into.

What I am about to give you in the next chapter is probably the most valuable information you can obtain before you invest in a mobile home park or any other type of real estate. Having grown up in a low-income family, the importance of cash flow became increasingly evident to me. Due to my perspective on cash flow that began when I was a child, today I would rather purchase a property that has a net cash flow (pre-tax) of $5,000 per month than a $100,000 lump sum at any one time. Cash flow never goes out of style, while equity can evaporate over night.

Cash-flow analysis is based on the actual cash flow— dollars in, dollars out.

Due to fear and intimidation of math, most people consider cash flow analysis to be rocket science, but it's actually quite simple. Every property I have ever purchased, and there are many, was purchased based on seventh-grade math. I have met so many people who say they do not like math. Well, if you do not become comfortable with running the numbers, you will not likely have the fortune of seeing significant numbers in your back account.

Before we begin, it is important to know when running numbers that we are concerned only with *actual numbers*. The term *actual* in this context means the amount of money legitimately coming in and the amount of money legitimately going out. Many times you will find property values based on *pro forma* values. *Pro forma* is what could be or what might be. Simply put, I buy a property for what it is, not what it could be. You must remember, if it was easy to make pro forma the actual number, the seller would have already done it. The key is to make sure you have the correct input items when running the numbers. Remember, like any mathematical formula, put garbage in and you will get garbage out.

We are about to go through several formulas that will assist you in performing financial analysis on an investment property that you are considering. The key to making those equations work is to run your numbers based on actual and current numbers. If the property brings in $3,500 per month, it will not help you to run numbers based on the potential income of $5,000. Cash-flow analysis is based on the actual cash flow—dollars in, dollars out. You can consider the potential "dollars in" later on.

To assist you in performing the following analysis, we have provided several tools, including spreadsheets and calculators, on the Trailer Cash website at www.trailercash.com.

Before we proceed into financial analysis, we must first discuss a topic that can, and will, blur the line between profiting in a transaction and losing money. The topic is emotions. Getting emotional is the fastest way to lose money in a transaction,

Do not allow your emotions into your investment decisions. Do the numbers.

period. I buy property to serve others and to make money. I meet a lot of people who are passionate about helping others but hurt themselves in the process. It's simple math: helping someone (+1) and hurting yourself (-1) equals zero net growth (0) in this world. It is a wonderful thing to serve another person, but you need to keep your other goal in perspective, and that is the need to be profitable. In the end, profitability leads to the ability to be charitable.

Chapter 6

Know Your Business

As with anything, there is risk in not knowing what you're doing. Like any business, you must build safety guards and systems. A pilot does not take off without a checklist, and you shouldn't try to get your business off the ground without one, either. Cash-flow analysis is another step in the process of investing that we utilize to minimize our risk. It is important to remind you that we only buy a property that is profitable on day one, so the ability to perform cash-flow analysis is imperative.

So let's get into some numbers here.

Cash-Flow Analysis Formulas

Success begins by recognizing value and moving fast to realize the opportunity that seeing such value brings. For example, if you saw a penny on the side of a walkway, you might just walk past it, but had it been a $100 bill, you would have quickly swooped down to pick it up. Seeing value in a potential acquisition is no different. If you wait even a day, the chances grow of another investor moving in on your deal.

Cash-flow analysis gives you a clear picture of a property's value by quantifying it based on its actual income and expenses. Cash-flow analysis is essentially an algebraic formula in which all the variables are added together so you can make a quick assessment of your potential return on capital and return on leverage. It either equals positive cash flow or not. It can also identify key areas in the income and expenses that can transform an acquisition into a positive, cash-flowing asset quickly or increase its current cash-flow position. It simplifies the decision-making process, reducing it down to a simple formula for success.

During your efforts to find a property, you collected the information on a park's income and expenses. Now it's time to examine those numbers more closely so that you can derive two very important numbers: the capitalization rate and the cash-on-cash return—two ways to determine the property's return on investment.

What Is Capitalization Rate?

Before we discuss what capitalization rate is and how to use it, we must first define many of the variables that make up the capitalization rate formula.

Capitalization rate = Annual net operating income / purchase price

Net operating income is the amount left over after fixed costs and variable costs are subtracted from gross rental income. Or, in other words, operating income is what you have left over when all expenses are paid. (This does not include the mortgage expense.)

Cash-flow analysis is essentially an algebraic formula in which all the variables are added together so you can make a quick assessment of your potential return.

Purchase price is the price you determine to sell an asset for if you are the seller or to purchase an asset for if you are the buyer. If you are simply looking at buying a property but have not agreed on an actual purchase price yet, you can use the asking price while you run the numbers for now.

Capitalization rate is the return on borrowed money (capital), assuming 100 percent of the property is financed. I have found that the meaning of capitalization rate typically confuses people. Simply put, if your borrowing costs are 7 percent, then you would logically want to make more than the costs of borrowing. A good spread would be 3 percent or more than the interest you are paying your lender. For example, if you buy a property and obtain financing at 7 percent interest, the capitalization rate you would want is 10 percent or greater.

Once again, the written formula to determine the capitalization rate is:

Capitalization rate = Annual net operating income / purchase price

This means the capitalization rate equals the net operating income divided by the purchase price. Sometimes this is called the *return on borrowed money.*

Don't let this equation scare you. You may not be a math geek, but don't check out on me now. Learning the few equations in this chapter and what they mean (combined with action) has the potential to make you very wealthy. Remember, seventh-grade math is all it takes.

Let's run through an example with simple numbers to practice figuring out and understanding capitalization rate. If a mobile home park is purchased for $1,000,000 (that's the purchase price) and it produces $100,000 in actual net operating income annually, then it would give you a 10 percent capitalization rate (that's $100,000 divided by $1,000,000).

$100,000 / $1,000,000 = .10 = 10 percent

If this same property were purchased for $500,000 with the same net income, then the capitalization rate would be:

$$\$100,000 / \$500,000 = .20 = 20 \text{ percent}$$

If you are then able to obtain financing for 7 percent, it would mean you would be earning 3 percent more than the cost of borrowing. Again, your goal should be to have your capitalization rate at least 3 percent higher than your interest rate. For example, if you have an interest rate of 11 percent, then you would want a 14 percent or greater capitalization rate in year one.

Note: As we are describing capitalization rate as the return on borrowed money, it is important to cover the instance of an investor acquiring property with cash. In the event that an investor acquires a property using cash, then the capitalization rate would be the same as the cash-on-cash return (see below), due to the fact that the cash invested would equal the amount the investor "financed" the property with his or her own cash.

What Is Cash-on-Cash Return?

Cash-on-cash return is another item we look at when making an investment. The basic description of cash-on-cash return is the amount of return on invested capital.

Cash-on-cash return = Annual net income / capital invested

For example, if a property produces $10,000 per year of net income (actual take-home income after all expenses are paid, including the mortgage) and the investor put $100,000 down, the cash-on-cash return is 10 percent. This metric can be used to compare what a real-estate investment would do compared to other investments.

$$\$10,000 / \$100,000 = .10 = 10 \text{ percent}$$

Formulas for Success

I want you to look at the capitalization rate equation one more time. Memorize it, practice it, and get comfortable with it.

Capitalization rate = Annual net operating income / purchase price

Let's take the equation we use to determine our capitalization rate and look at it a few different ways.

Capitalization rate = Annual net operating income / purchase price

Annual net operating income = Purchase price *x* capitalization rate

Purchase price = Annual net operating income / capitalization rate

Once you plug the numbers that you have into these formulas, you will be able to solve for the missing item. For example, let's say you know what the net operating income is and you know what capitalization rate you are willing to have to make a purchase. You can then solve for the purchase price.

It is also important to note that when you put a property under contract, you will often find through the due-diligence process that the numbers provided during negotiations were not correct. The reality of a deal being a little different than you originally thought it would be is not unusual—and it does not have to be a deal breaker. In fact, these variations, in many cases, provide the needed leverage to take an acquisition from good to great. It is important to note that, as the due-diligence process takes place after an accepted offer, the seller is typically more inclined to agree to changes in the due-diligence portion of the transaction than if you pre-negotiate the transaction.

Let me give you an example. When you place a property under contract, you are saying you're interested in acquiring the property. Many people think that making an offer is an absolute, and it doesn't have to be, assuming you are using a well-formed contract. At the time of acceptance, many sellers begin imagining what they can buy with their newfound wealth and begin to spend their "mental money." If at some point in the due-diligence process you find something was not disclosed or is different than you thought, you can then renegotiate the transaction to account for your new findings. The willingness of the seller to renegotiate at this point in time usually comes from the potential loss of the items they have purchased with the "mental money" they will receive at closing. As Donald Trump has said, "Ninety-nine percent of all negotiation happens after the contract is signed."

We will get into how to identify differences when we discuss due diligence. If any numbers change during your due-diligence phase, plug in the new numbers and see if it still makes sense. I'll give you an example so you can track with me on recalculating a property's value after a change in the selling price or actual numbers during the due-diligence check.

Here is a simple, common pro forma scenario:

- Seller asks $400,000 for property

- Seller claims property generates $5,000 net operating income per month ($60,000 annually)

- $60,000 / $400,000 = 15 percent capitalization rate

Reality:

- Seller asks $400,000 for property

- Due diligence finds the property only nets $3,000 per month ($36,000 annually), due to expenses not being factored and other items

- $36,000 / $400,000 = 9 percent capitalization rate

The difference between what the seller said the property makes and the reality of what it actually makes can make the difference between an OK deal and a great deal. We will talk about due diligence later in the book, but it is important to know that it impacts that value and the purchase price.

Gold Nugget

It is smart business to base your purchase price offer on your desired capitalization rate. If the seller has set the purchase price so high that you cannot achieve your desired capitalization rate and will not budge, the deal is a "no go." The asking price could also be too low to resist, in which case it's a "we're on!" In these cases, which occur more often than you would imagine, you must be ready to take action quickly. Failure to move will most likely result in someone else capturing the opportunity you may have seen first.

Again, I want to stress—always run *your* numbers. A very important fact to understand is that the capitalization rate can look very different when you view it from the seller's perspective versus the buyer's perspective. What a seller may provide as the capitalization rate may not be the actual capitalization rate a buyer will experience. Not only do sellers have different expenses than you will in many cases, but the purchase price they have in mind may not be what you settle on in negotiations. The point, once again, is to always run your own numbers. Always. It doesn't matter who refers a deal to me or how much I trust them. Anyone can make a mistake. If I purchase a property, it is my responsibility, regardless of whether I ran the numbers or not.

Be sure to have a clear understanding of all income and expenses before proceeding. I have provided an analysis tool that will assist you in running your numbers. To use this tool, please visit www.trailercash.com.

What Is a Good Cap Rate?

If you think of it as the return on borrowed capital, a good capitalization rate will be higher than the interest you're paying. It varies, depending on your personal goals and timeframe, but I have heard it taught that a 10 percent or greater capitalization rate represents a good buy. However, I disagree.

The problem I have with this logic is due to the simple fact that a static figure is being taught in a dynamic world. If capitalization is a return on borrowed capital and today's interest rates on commercial real estate are in the 6–8 percent range, then, yes, a 10 percent capitalization rate would be good. The problem occurs when and if inflation rears its head. Then the Federal Reserve will likely raise interest rates to combat inflation.

Let's say interest rates rise to 12 percent in the future. Operating under the premise that a 10 percent capitalization rate is good is no longer the case. As previously mentioned, I feel it is better to look for a spread of 3 percent or more than the interest rate you are obtaining for your financing. For example, if you were to purchase a property and obtain a rate of 11 percent on the financing, you would then seek a capitalization rate of 14 percent or more.

The higher the cap rate, the better. We have purchased properties with a cap rate of 15 percent or better. This isn't to say that every deal will perform at this level, but it is important to know that this has been achieved consistently. The more you know about and the more experience you have in the asset class, the easier it will become to maximize the performance of a property.

The capitalization rate levels the cash-flow analysis playing field, so to speak, because

> As a rule of thumb, if you're making 2–3 percent more than you're paying the bank, that's a good cap rate.

it does not factor your interest rate or mortgage payment into the scenario, which could vary from buyer to buyer. Instead, it compares the income, expenses, and price or value of the property.

How Do I Know if It's a Good Deal?

While the capitalization rate is your return on the bank's money, the cash-on-cash return is your return on your own money invested into the property. Many people who are new to investing commonly ask, "How do I know what kind of return I'm looking for?" That is a good question, and the answer largely depends on the individual's financial situation.

Let's say you have $100,000 sitting in a savings account, 401K, or IRA. How much are you making on that $100,000 annually? Some of you might either laugh or cry at that question, based on what we have sadly seen people's retirement accounts do, but that is a reasonable starting point of comparison.

If you can have your cash sitting in an account that makes 2–3 percent per year, barely above the inflation rate, or you can invest it into a deal that produces 20 percent return on your investment in the first year, what would you rather do?

I was recently working with an elderly woman, and we were discussing her financial situation. Her husband had passed away over ten years before. They had lived a great life together, and her husband had left her approximately $1 million in a retirement account when he died. This was a blessing for her and her children. She asked me to look at her account with her, and we studied it together. Her approximate balance was still about $1 million.

She thought she was doing good because her advisors hadn't lost any of her money. The reality is that the only people making money off of what she and her husband had built were the advisors, through all of their fees. Considering inflation alone, let's say she had $1 million in her account on January 1, 2000, and over the course of the next ten years she didn't make or lose anything, so that at January 1, 2010, she still had $1 million in her account. Due to inflation, though, the value of her $1 million had dropped to nearly $650,000 in 2010. That is a loss of nearly 35 percent!

It is important for you to know that not losing money as a goal is losing money against inflation over time. If you think inflation will rise in the future, then this scenario will get worse for those whose money is sitting on the sidelines.

The Name of the Game

The name of this profit game is *cash-on-cash return*. This is the key to unlocking the profit potential of your chosen investment. This equation determines your return on invested capital—what you put in up front, if anything.

To derive your cash-on-cash return, simply divide the amount of the first year's net income by the amount of cash you invested. For example, if you put $100,000 down on a deal and you make $20,000 net in your first year, you had a 20 percent cash-on-cash return in the first year. Not bad, but we want you to think about this a little more creatively. What if you made that $20,000 net with only $1,000 of your own money invested? That's a bit more than 20 percent cash-on-cash return, isn't it? The trick is to use more brainpower than money.

Figuring out your desired cash-on-cash return ahead of time is "beginning with the end in mind." You will know the answer to the question, "How do I know if it's a good deal?" because you will have established the benchmark for performance up front. Cash-on-cash return lets you compare the property to other cash investments.

In the above example, you invested $100,000 cash in a property that paid 20 percent in the first year. If one-year certificates of deposit (CDs) were paying 20 percent, you'd likely prefer the security of banking the money. But if CDs are paying 3 percent, there's no comparison. That is why a friend of mine calls them "Certificates of Death and Depreciation."

Perhaps you are starting with very little cash or no cash. A no-money-down deal can be done, maybe not at the frequency we might all hope, but these types of deals can still be structured. You may also be in a situation where you are not investing your own cash but are partnering with someone who is putting his or her money into the deal. We can figure out the cash-on-cash return for the individual investing. However, if you are putting zero of your own money into the deal, you are essentially getting an infinite rate of return on your investment.

As I meet people all over the country while speaking at conventions and conferences alike, one of the biggest excuses I hear from people who have thought about investing in real estate is, "I don't have any money to invest." My response is always the same, and that is, "Don't use it!" It is fascinating to recognize that most millionaires I know use very little of their own money as investment capital. Their wealth is a byproduct of their competence in the marketplace and their ability and willingness to serve others with a quality product. The rich are rich because they know how to effectively leverage their knowledge rather than their checkbook on every deal. The poor are poor because when they have the cash, they usually spend it. Many Americans spend more on Christmas presents than their own education and furthering their knowledge.

I cannot say what amount of profit satisfies *your* business objectives. Most people would not borrow money at 15 percent if they could help it, but I would happily borrow at 15 percent if I could deposit the money at the same bank and earn 20 percent. It's the return that matters most.

Before you start investing, decide what your target is and work toward that. Investing in mobile home parks has been an area of investment opportunity where we have seen the highest consistent cash-on-cash returns in real estate. A 20 percent cash-on-cash return is something that is reasonable to achieve through investing in mobile home parks. A consistent, systematic approach to running your business will establish consistency and growth in your return on investment.

Many of those friends who questioned my sanity when I first started in real estate are now coming to my husband and I with tight finances, curious about our business model. We are thrilled to be able to help at this point, and I understand their initial trepidation. I have seen how many people become so consumed with fear and impacted by the negative comments from their social group that they never take the first step toward their own financial success. I will offer you a concept I live by, and that is: if someone in your life cannot tell you what to do, then they have no right to tell you what not to do, either. It is unfortunate to see how many potential entrepreneurs are talked out of starting by those who are threatened by their actions and potential success. Do not succumb to this, as it is more common than you think.

Now that Ryan and I have set all our systems in place, it is a solid business with very, if any, unknown factors. We have taken out the fear factor by using a consistent due diligence and management system. As I keep trying to hammer home, we only buy properties that are making money from the first day of ownership. How much more conservative can you get than buying property with a proven track record that pays you the day you close?

Potential Expenses

We have talked about the basic investment formulas for capitalization rate and cash-on-cash return. We have talked about their definitions and what they mean. This next section is going to elaborate a bit more about the details that make up those formulas. This might be something that is dry to read for informational purposes, but it actually represents many key points where people make mistakes. They don't really know what is considered a part of the income and the expenses that make up net operating income. We are going to go through that a bit here, so hang on!

Some people get woozy just looking at the list, assuming it must cost a fortune to run a mobile home park. That is not necessarily the case, and it certainly isn't the point. Every business will have expenses—the important thing is to know what they are and to learn how to minimize them without devaluing the business. Some of these expenses may never come into play, but if they do, you will need to include them while running the numbers. I'll list a few here to get you going. For a full list of possible expenses for a mobile home park, please visit www.trailercash.com.

Advertising

Advertising is required to increase and maintain occupancy rates. The current owner may or may not have incurred or tracked costs, but you may expect to spend something like 0–5 percent of gross income on average, depending on vacancy rates. It is important to note that the bulk of your tenants will come from drive-bys. This means you need to invest in a quality sign at the front of your community. Great signage is key and is an excellent advertising source.

Insurance for liability, property, and workers' compensation

These vary by market. Contact a reputable insurance agent to provide a quote for what it will cost to properly insure your future investment. This is an area I watch people try to skimp on, and it could literally cost you hundreds of thousands of dollars if you do not take this seriously. Property insurance is an investment in peace of mind and can definitely save your assets in the case of a natural disaster, so just do it.

Mortgage interest

Mortgage interest is not actually part of the capitalization rate calculation, but it's a real expense that you must pay, so be sure to include it in your cash-flow analysis.

Maintenance, labor, and supplies

Maintenance, labor, and supplies can vary dramatically from property to property and can also be different from owner to owner. The biggest difference is whether or not the mobile homes are owned by the park or owned by the tenant. If the homes are owned by the tenant, you are in a land-lease position, which is very attractive from an expense standpoint. On the other hand, if the mobile homes are owned by the park, the expense can be as high as 10 percent.

Maintenance, labor, and material costs are not only high because of the day-to-day wear-and-tear on the mobile home. There can also be significant costs when tenants move in and out. If someone owns his or her own home, turnover in a mobile home park is significantly reduced.

Property taxes

Property taxes can range between 1–3 percent of assessed value depending on where the property is located. You can always call the tax assessor or visit their website to get the correct information. Get the right figure and build it into your cash-flow estimates. Remember that the current owner may give you their figure, but yours might be much higher after reassessment. Be sure to understand how the property will be valued after you acquire it.

Utilities—electric, gas, trash, water, and sewer

It is essential to know who pays for what and how you might change that upon taking ownership. It bears repeating that utilities are one of the biggest profit leaks in mobile home parks. Transferring responsibility for utilities to the tenants not only plugs a potential profit leak in your collections but also gets you out of the utility business altogether, transferring utility issues and expenses to the utility company and the tenant.

Phone and internet

Budget $100–$150 per month for phone, internet, and fax. We prefer to set up the phone service and then forward that to the manager's cell phone. We do not provide the managers with a cell phone, as we have learned that although you can't imagine they would need to make international calls on your phone, your manager may see it differently. Also, it is easier to transition away from a manager when it is time to replace the manager. Simply stop the calls from forwarding to the manager's phone and redirect it to a number of your choice.

You might bring phone costs down with a Vonage account forwarded to your manager's cell phone. You need an account you can monitor and a number that stays with the park if the manager leaves.

Good management

Good management is perhaps the most important expense of all, and the most worth it. Whatever the previous owners were spending on management, odds are you will be spending a different amount. Bear that in mind so you can reserve a budget for it. We will cover management and its cost in a later section.

Think Like a Lender

Now, keeping all of your potential expenses in mind, think about how you can balance out the cash-flow analysis in your favor. Think of ways to increase your cap rate. Think like a lender.

Understanding how mobile home parks are valued will help you create great deals and be a more effective negotiator. Generally speaking, a park's valuation formula takes the number of occupied lots, multiplies that by the average lot rent, and then applies a multiplier to establish the land value. If the park pays for the utilities, the multiplier is 60. If tenants are responsible for their own utilities, the multiplier is 70. This creates cash flow and profit opportunities.

Let's look at an example of a park with fifty occupied lots. In this case, let's say the park pays for the utilities and the average lot rent at this park is $125 but average lot rent in the market is $150. That means we have two opportunities to significantly increase the value of the park, first in passing on the cost of utilities to the tenants and second by increasing the lot rent to fair-market value.

- Park pays sewer and water:

    Occupied lots x average lot rent x 60 = Park value
    50 x $125 x 60 = $375,000 value

- Residents pay sewer and water:

    Occupied lots x average lot rent x 70 = Park value
    50 x $125 x 70 = $437,500 value

If we spend $37,500 to individually meter each unit so the residents pay their own utilities ($750 x 50), the value of the property increases by $62,500, for an immediate net gain of $25,000.

But what if we also increased the rent to the market average of $150?

$$50 \times \$150 \times 70 = \$525,000 \text{ value}$$

Master this equation the way a waiter calculates tips: instantly and correctly. When you're on the phone with a prospective seller and he asks $375,000 for this property, you know that's a reasonable selling price and you still have opportunities to increase the cash flow and value. If he asks for $300,000, you're running for the fax machine to get that offer into his hands.

While you're thinking like a lender, don't forget to think like a landlord. You cannot be reluctant to raise rents. You're looking for properties that are currently charging less than fair-market rent, as you will have the opportunity to increase your income immediately.

A Word about Seller Information

Whether it's ignorance, exaggeration, or straight-up fibbing, it doesn't really matter. Taking an owner at his word and basing your decision on his calculations is like cheating on a math test and then blaming the guy whose answers you copied when you fail the test. Make it easy on yourself—do your first cash-flow analysis based on their numbers but assume you will get incorrect numbers. Do your own research and redo your math equations if any new variables arise.

From the seller's perspective, he is just trying to paint a flattering picture of the park's income generation. Plus, it should almost go without saying: sellers don't always keep the most scrupulous records. We have been presented rent rolls on the back of envelopes and been grateful because at least it's better than the park owners who collect rent in cash and throw wads of money into the glove compartment of a pickup truck and have no rent roll records. When talking to owners, it is surprising the number of owners don't actually know the number of pads at their park, for example, and estimate in both directions. Nowadays, you can look at the location on Google Earth and count the pads from the comfort of your own desk. When you come across a disorganized owner or manager, consider it your advantage. Their misinformation will likely be a point you can use in your favor during negotiations.

What if an owner tells you the park has full occupancy and then you discover on your visit that you count thirty-three unoccupied lots at the same park? How much would it cost to achieve 80 or 90 or 100 units x $150 x 70? Keep running the numbers. Your ability to do your own cash-flow analysis will give you a professional investor's confidence. Now you can truly appreciate the value. You're getting closer to locking in on the deal of a lifetime. So let's get you equipped to turn this newfound opportunity into a great deal with a winning purchase agreement.

> When you come across a disorganized owner or manager, consider it your advantage. Their misinformation will likely be a point you can use in your favor during negotiations.

Count on Exponential Expansion

I want to remind you that this book is not only about getting wealthier; it's also about serving others and taking them with you. When you formally decide what your financial goals are, you will need to define your approach and timeline and determine what it will take to achieve your goals. In other words, if you want to achieve big things, you have to think even bigger and be willing to take big action. Many people are out there trying to make money in real estate one unit at a time. They are going, "One, two, three, four, five, six, seven, eight, nine, ten." When they get to ten units, though, they end up quitting because they are overwhelmed with all of the time it takes to manage those ten units. This growth pattern of one at a time is a linear model of expansion and is intrinsically flawed.

Part of what we do is re-teach the investors we work with how to think in terms of, "One, two, three, four, thirty, ninety, two hundred, one thousand." If you start out doing onesies and twosies like Ryan and I did, then consider the fact that one mobile home park is sometimes the same price as one or two average single-family homes. Suddenly you begin to wonder why you have been building your portfolio one unit at a time.

At first you might panic: "Thirty?! That's too large of a property. I can't handle that many units!" But the reality is, managing thirty units is very similar to managing twenty units. You will now be benefiting from the economies of scale on the expense side of things and enjoying a higher net profit per pad.

As you decide to expand your business, there are going to naturally be constraints on your time that you will have to manage. With that in mind, here is a way that we were able to increase our growth exponentially.

Leverage Your Time

After doing the cold calls myself for quite sometime, I knew that I could leverage my time better by hiring someone else to do the up-front calls and research so that I could focus more on negotiating deals and managing the managers. Ryan and I were looking forward to the growth of our business and were excited to bring in others who could benefit from what we were building.

The work we needed done at the time was not something that would require someone with an MBA or significant amount of experience, but we knew we were going to have to train whoever we brought in this niche market of real estate. Considering the people available to perform this job, we ended up hiring the same woman who had trained me several years earlier in my first job as the hostess at Steak & Ale! I trusted her, and I knew she had a great work ethic. I also knew the income she would be able to earn by working with us would have a substantial impact on her family, and it was fun to realize this was an opportunity to make so much more than we ever did at that restaurant.

Dana was our first part-time hire. We set her up in her own home office so she could take her son to school and then come home and work with us on building out our mobile home park business. We trained her on what she needed to know and got her going. She ended up helping us close three park deals within approximately the first eighteen months! On just her second deal, she earned $39,000! She and her family were able to use that, along with the profit from the other deals, to tackle some accrued debt and other investments, plus use the profit toward her son's tuition. It was a blessing to see firsthand the domino effect that success can have on people's lives. Not too bad for a part-time job and working, stay-at-home mom!

For Dana and her family, this one deal was life changing. For us, the effect was exponential. It not only meant hundreds more rent checks into our account each month, but also it confirmed for us a dream we had talked about trying to create from the start—that our buying MHPs could effectively equip others with their own financial success.

Dana had earned it—we didn't just hand her a check—and it built her confidence in what she could do for herself in the future. Sometimes when I am speaking to a room of several hundred individuals, knowing that so many are struggling financially, it is encouraging to me to think of the people like Dana who have been positively affected by applied knowledge in the marketplace. I want each person I speak to or meet to know they have the ability to change their life by taking the time to learn how to do this, and then, more importantly, by implementing what they have learned. I have to say that this entire process was incredibly gratifying.

This first growth spurt of our business was such a revelation for us. We saw that we were setting up our business model so that we could effectively grow, as well as impact the lives of others in a positive way. We quickly grew to three stay-at-home moms and beyond, helping us go from two...to ten...to fifty...to over fourteen hundred home sites. They needed the extra income and flexibility of working from home, and we needed the help making initial contacts with park owners. These were not charity cases, though. Believe me, these ladies were motivated, and they performed. The cash-flow analysis we have discussed in this chapter is the foundation for our growth.

Chapter 7

The Contract—
Get It in Writing

How did you feel when you bought your first car or your first home—excited? Nervous? Signing your name to any contract will most likely create a level of fear and excitement. As you build your business, there will be a lot less fear and a lot more excitement.

One aspect in my life that is a non-negotiable is having ethics in all I do. If you are not going to honor an agreement, don't put your name on it. On the flip side, just because you are going to honor your word doesn't mean the other person will—get everything in writing.

A major stumbling point for many investors comes from the perception that putting a property under contract means you are actually buying the property. We need to talk about what it means when you put a property under contract. First, what it does not mean is that you are automatically going to be purchasing the property that has been placed under contract. This point is for the inexperienced investor. Many newbies are afraid to put a property under contract because they do not want to get stuck with a property that is not a good deal. As I mentioned before, Donald Trump is noted for saying, "All negotiation begins after the contract has been signed." Whether you love him or hate him, that remark is true. In this chapter, we are going to talk about many of the aspects to contracting that you need to know before putting a property under contract.

I know people who have gotten this far in their pursuit of a better life only to abruptly stop because they were afraid to sign their names to a contract. Most of the time, the reason they get nervous is because they assume their signature on the contract is binding them to the purchase of the property. Please don't be that person! You are still in the process of turning a good opportunity into a great deal. That means you are proposing a deal by putting your best offer and terms in writing. Period.

A contract, when executed, becomes a legal document that is binding. In fact, getting the deal in writing will save you from all kinds of unnecessary issues. However, that doesn't mean that just because you sign your name, you are buying the property.

Before we proceed, it is very important to discuss contingency clauses. The clauses allow you to put a property under contract and have the ability to get you out of the agreement if you find something that is unacceptable to you. Most newbies are fearful of placing a property under contract because they do not have a clear idea of what contingencies to account for. I don't blame them! It's the classic question of, "How do I know what I don't know?"

If I was placing a property under contract with zero contingencies before having a chance to perform my due diligence, I'd be fearful as well! This would be like buying a car and then taking it on a test drive—not a good idea. In order to test drive a property, we must put it under contract, then review, and then make a final decision on whether or not to purchase.

Think of a contract as simply a representation of whatever two people agree to in writing. For you, the buyer, a contract simply locks up what you believe to be the situation:

1. I agree to buy this specific mobile home park.

2. I agree upon this price at this time until said closing date.

3. The mobile home park must meet this set of conditions, and if not, I am able to cancel the agreement or renegotiate.

The Seller's Perspective

As in any sport, knowing how the game is played is imperative, but knowing how the opponent thinks is king! I will share some insights that I have learned over the years in the hopes that it can help you in your business.

When you make first contact with a potential seller and begin discussing your intent to purchase his or her property, they begin to envision their retirement, that car they always wanted, or simply a full set of teeth (if you believe the stigmas).

The simple fact is this: once you start discussing money, people start spending it. That means the further you progress into the deal, the more motivated the seller tends to become. Imagine that you are just two weeks from closing and the seller is not willing to renegotiate based on items you discovered in your due-diligence process. You may proceed, knowing what you have found, or you

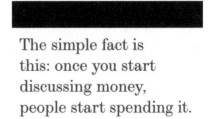

The simple fact is this: once you start discussing money, people start spending it.

may want to cancel the contract utilizing one of the contingency clauses you have placed in your contract.

In the event that you threaten to cancel the contract, the seller has to come to terms with the loss of all of the "mental items" they purchased with their "mental money" from the sale. While they have not yet laid hands on these items, they will begin to see them slip away. In many cases, I have found this to be a substantial negotiating factor in many of my transactions. I have learned that if you cannot walk away, you cannot negotiate. If you cannot negotiate, you will not end up with the best possible deal.

We put much of the property we purchase under contract, sight unseen. To the inexperienced individual, that may sound like a stretch or just plain foolish, but the reality is, we purchase property all over the country and we don't have the time or desire to be onsite for every offer. Just because we are putting a property under contract doesn't mean we are going to end up purchasing it. With our research team looking for property, we could put out multiple offers on multiple properties in the same week. It would not be time- or cost-efficient to be onsite at all these properties in the same week. We feel comfortable doing this because our contract is structured with the proper contingency clauses.

We are in the business of acquiring properties. We are not going to overpay, and we are never going to buy something other than what we intend to purchase. This way, we can sleep well at night knowing we have taken the appropriate precautions in the purchasing process, and we do not have to stay up worrying about the what-ifs.

A Good Contract Will Save Your Assets

We were pleased that our very first mobile home park acquisition went off without a hitch. Our second purchase became a huge lesson in how thoroughly our contracts and documents were helping or not helping us. It also became the impetus for putting together our 52-point due-diligence checklist, which we will discuss more later in the book.

During our second mobile home park acquisition, we signed a contract for a park where the seller falsified all his rent rolls. He provided falsified supporting information as well and even signed a statement verifying that all information provided was correct. We bought that park for $450,000, with the seller taking back $80,000 in seller financing.

After we bought the property, we found blatant evidence the park did not actually produce the income he claimed when we agreed to buy it. We had done everything we could to prevent this situation by checking their income statements and reviewing the necessary documents in the due-diligence phase, but the owner had coerced his accountant to sign off on his fraudulent numbers—numbers that represented the park's "potential" income, not "actual" income as stated in the contract. What saved us from losing on the deal? The contract had his signature avowing his statements had been true and accurate: that became an $80,000 signature! I knew we could get him to forgive the $80,000 part of the loan he was financing because he and the CPA had so obviously made fraudulent claims. That piece of paper was not our trap but our leverage to renegotiate, even after we already owned the property.

Getting the deal in writing will save you from all kinds of unnecessary issues.

We confronted the owner privately to avoid a major battle because we both knew he had clearly committed fraud. We let him know we could sue him for falsifying statements to us and the lender and that, even if we didn't sue him, the lender would likely take legal action because the bank based their loan on those "signed and certified" rent rolls. He knew we were actually saving him from being sued by the lender. Rather than go to court and face potentially greater penalties, he forgave the $80,000 note he had financed.

This reduction in the total cost made it a great deal again. The quality of the deal was restored. In fact, we came out ahead! We then set out to improve the value by improving occupancy and income, making the property what it was presented to be when we purchased it. The opportunity to turn this losing deal into a winning deal would not have been possible had we not had the proper documents signed and in place to protect us. In the end, our objective is to profit, not to be right or vindicated. *(Note: Nothing in this book should be considered legal advice, and we highly recommend you work with a trusted lawyer to craft your contracts.)*

Our purchase-and-sale agreement and due-diligence documents provided a standardized approach that gave us all the recourse we needed to get the deal we wanted. We were able to turn that situation around to our advantage without bringing in a team of lawyers or taking him to court because of one single provision in our due-diligence checklist—that the seller sign a statement stating that all information provided is true and factual and certifies the rent rolls. If he doesn't stick to his end of the bargain, you are no longer obligated to stick to yours.

Contract Essentials

Now that you've seen an example, you can see the importance of getting your contract in writing and signed. Don't go to some random website and download a cheap $5 contract. You will need to make an investment in your contract. This is every bit as important as a carpenter investing in his tools. In fact, at this point I have invested tens of thousands in legal documents for our business, and it has been worth every penny, if not more.

With every property we have purchased, we have learned another lesson. While our contract is too intricate—and frankly, too valuable—to share in its entirety here, we can still discuss some of the more important clauses.

Due-diligence clause

In a nutshell, due diligence is the process of making sure you are getting what it is you think you have found. Due diligence is the most important pre-purchase protection you've got, and I would never sign a contract that didn't have a provision for due diligence. The due-diligence process can seem a little tedious for sellers at times because all they really care about is selling the property. They are not as interested in providing all of the detailed information that we require. However, we clearly communicate that we cannot close until we have done a proper evaluation of their property. We also mention that the sooner we are able to verify all of the information we request during our due-diligence period, the sooner they get paid. This gets everyone on the same page and working toward the common goal—a closing.

As a buyer, you should know what information you are going to require during your due-diligence period. If you are able, go ahead and start gathering some of this with the seller as you are working through the negotiations. As you gain experience, you will also understand that the more information you gather, the more you can negotiate. However, don't attempt to do full due diligence on a deal without having it under contract. I have seen many new investors try to perform due diligence on a deal they don't even have under contract. At the end of the day, if the property is not under contract, you have nothing. Be sure to control the asset (through the contract) before doing all the work. We've made a simple purchase-and-sale agreement available for you online at www.trailercash.com.

People sometimes pay third parties to perform due diligence for them, and it costs thousands of dollars for someone's knowledge, time, and expertise. Still, at the end of the day, *you* are the person responsible as the investor to understand the due-diligence information because you're the one benefiting or not benefiting from the property. Performing due diligence properly can make or break the investment. My husband and I hold seminars where we work through our complete due-diligence list with investors, as well as many other topics not discussed in this book on account of time. See www.trailertrash.com to see if and when we will be teaching in your area. For now, just remember that the due-diligence clause is written into the contract so that, in the end, you get what you are paying for. It's nobody's job but the buyer's to make sure that the due-diligence clause is written into the contract.

It is important to note again that just because you discover something in the due-diligence process that isn't exactly as you thought, that doesn't mean it is a deal breaker. While there are items out there that can be discovered during the due-diligence process that would call for immediate cancellation, the due-diligence process can be a great opportunity for negotiating.

Subject to suitable financing

Whether you use a bank or seller financing, make sure you can get out of the deal if the money is not there. This is essential! A bad situation can be avoided by four words: *subject to suitable financing*. *Suitable* means whatever is suitable to the buyer.

Subject to partner's approval

We include "subject to partner's approval" as a kind of safety valve, as well, that gives us another escape if something about the deal starts to look wrong to us, even beyond the due-diligence period. The subtlety is in the definition of terms, because if you have a partner—and you don't have to define your partner; it could tech-nically be anyone—and if "subject to partner's approval" is not defined along a timeline, then "subject to partner's approval" can extend up until the day of closing, and your partner could not agree the day before. Technically, then, a "partner's" lack of approval of the deal going through constitutes a legal reason to cancel and get your deposit back. It's not exactly a get-out-of-jail-free card, but it's an extra layer of safety after the due-diligence clause and "subject to suitable financing." Again, it is our desire to close on income-producing properties, but it is important to fully utilize contingency clauses to properly protect yourself in case the property is not what was reported by the seller.

Assignment of contract—a big gold nugget

This clause gives you the power to assign the contract to another buyer and keep the deal locked in. You might find an outstanding deal at a time when you are not ready to act on it or an excellent deal that doesn't really fit your business model but would be a great deal for someone else. This strategy is great for investors starting out with little money or credit. If you know what you're doing, you can leverage your knowledge. Remember, *you* are getting wealthier by thinking smarter.

In these cases, I identify myself as the buyer by putting "Jamie Smith and/or assigns" in the buyer's line of the contract. As is common when purchasing a property through a real-estate professional, many times you will find that buried in the agreement it states something to the effect that "this contract is not assignable." You may be asking yourself, "How can I assign a contract that is not assignable?" The answer is really quite simple. In a contract environment, typewritten supersedes preprinted documents, and handwriting supersedes all. So by simply handwriting your name in the buyer's line as "Your Name and/or assigns," you gain the ability to assign the contract to another party.

You may say, "Great! What does that mean?" Assigning a contract simply means you are transferring ownership of the agreement to another party, many times in exchange for a fee. The other party could be another investor or even another company that you own. Why would we do something like this? Sometimes we find a great deal, but maybe it's too small for our model or it's too far off the beaten track of where we are focusing our investment efforts. Then we might want to sell the deal to another buyer for an assignment fee. We still help the seller sell the property, we get paid for our up-front time and work, and another buyer gets a good deal that didn't happen to fit our business model. Theoretically, you could make a business out of assigning contracts, but that is not our intent. This is yet another strategy that helps us make the most of each opportunity. This is a unique strategy in that it doesn't require any cash and it doesn't require any credit, but it allows you to leverage your knowledge for compensation.

As an example, let's say you research and find a mobile home park that by your estimates produces $5,000 a month of net income, but due to credit, time, or monetary restrictions, you are unable to purchase the property yourself. Do you think anyone would be interested in the property you have found and placed under contract? Do you want the yes or the *heck yes*?

Having been the buyer and the seller of many agreements over the years, I have come up with a simple rule for valuing a contract. At this point in my business, I have decided that it would take ten months of net income for me to give up my position in a contract. So in this example:

$$\$5,000 \; x \; 10 = \$50,000$$

A common question I receive at this point is, "Where do we find people who want to buy contracts?" Think: where would you find a person who would invest $50,000 to net $5,000 per month? If you can't find anyone, you need a new group of friends, and if you don't have any friends, stop reading now and take a shower. It may help.

Let me ask you a few last questions. How much credit do you need to put a property under contract? How much money do you need to put a property under contract (read on if you don't know)? The answer to both of these questions is *none!* This is a clear example of how you can get this ball rolling no matter what financial position you are currently in. Like I have said, stop looking at the speed bump and get over it!

Prorated rents

By asking for prorated rents and then structuring our deals to close near the first of the month, we get a quick boost in income because rents are typically collected during the first week of the month. Rents are collected in advance, but expenses are paid in arrears, so we get the first month's revenue without the previous month's expenses. This is a very common expectation. Sellers will almost always go for it, but if you don't ask for it, you may not get it. We always ask for it.

Personal property

If you are buying a park with personal property included in the sale and you don't identify specifically what that personal property is, you may not get it. The seller could take everything you thought you were getting with them on the day of closing, and they would have every right to do so if you did not specifically identify it as a part of the sale. Many times at the time you execute the contract, you may not have all of the details of the personal property that you plan to acquire from the seller. In that case, you should generally state the personal property that you plan to acquire (including mobile homes, air conditioners, stoves, mowers, etc.) and state that the balance of the information associated with the personal property will be identified prior to the close of the due-diligence period.

Deal breakers

We are not married to a property that we put under contract. Here are reasons we've found to cancel contracts:

- Declining market—jobs are moving out of the area
- No reasonable financing available
- We discover the park is in a flood zone
- Failed phase one environmental

Of course, we don't draw the seller's attention to any section of the contract. When sellers are looking at a purchase-and-sale agreement, their eyes move to the price and the closing date. Oftentimes they do not review the contract in detail. This does not mean you are trying to pull anything over on the seller, but it is the reality of what you can expect. If a seller asks me about a clause, I can certainly explain it in terms that will not be offensive to him, but more often than not, the seller cares only about the price.

The event-driven contract

We utilize event-driven language in our contracts because it protects us from uncooperative or lackadaisical owners and from circumstances outside the owner's control or our control. Stuff happens—like slow appraisers, surveyors, and other third-party service providers. I learned about having event-driven language as part of our purchase-and-sale agreement as a result of repeatedly having appraisers and surveyors push us outside our due-diligence or contract period. We wanted to eliminate the concern of having the seller try to renegotiate with us for any reason when we needed to extend the due diligence or closing date. Here's one example of event-driven language: "The seller will provide to the buyer all requested items for due diligence [provide list] within 10 days of the extended contract or the due-diligence period will automatically be extended by 15 days." It is the desire of the buyer and the seller to close, but the buyer is the individual who needs to verify information before closing—the seller is just waiting to get paid at that point.

Another reason to use event-driven language in your documents is to avoid collusion between a service provider and the seller. In one case, before we knew any better, we chose an appraiser recommended by the seller, thinking we would benefit from a faster turnaround. As it turned out, the appraiser we hired told the owner she was crazy not to demand more for the property, so she told him to drag his feet on turning in the appraisal. All of a sudden, we were nearing the closing date and still did not have an appraisal complete. In order to finalize the loan, we worked with our lender to diligently push on the appraiser to get the job done, but it was clearly having no effect. We didn't have our appraisal and we could not get the owner or the appraiser to return our calls. We were eager to buy this park, partially because the selling price was so attractive. This was a big deal for us—the monthly net income was about $12,000 per month.

The seller provided all her other information, but now we were approaching the contract expiration date. We could not close because we had not yet gotten the appraisal back so that the lender could fund the deal. At that point, the seller demanded an exorbitant amount in addition to the agreed-upon purchase price or no deal. Needless to say, the answer was "no deal." Again, if you are not willing to walk, you have no leg to stand on in a negotiation. We walked. That was a significant waste of time, but we had to take our losses (time) and move on.

A great example of an event-driven contract comes from a friend of mine who is a developer in California. Back in the late 1980s, he had the opportunity to put a property under contract for roughly $2 million. In his agreement, he placed a clause that stated, "Closing to take place 30 days after development approval." It took nearly fourteen years to get approval for his project! He closed on this property in the early 2000s and had well over $5 million in equity the day of closing! Event-driven contracts are extremely common in the real-estate industry and are tools for many successful investors.

Consideration, and an alternative to cash

People I meet at conferences commonly ask me, "What is consideration?" To which I reply, "It's when my husband takes out the trash without me asking." All jokes aside, consideration goes by several names and is important in the contracting process. Consideration is also commonly known as an "earnest money deposit" or an "escrow deposit." No matter what it is called, you need it because without consideration you do not have a binding agreement.

Consideration is further defined as "anything of value." Notice it doesn't say money! I always love it when someone from the "I Don't Have's" group asks, "How can I get started if I don't have any money?" I always ask, "Why do you need it?" To which they typically reply, "I just assumed I did." Well, there's the issue right there. I always find it humorous when people perceive roadblocks that aren't even there.

Early on in our business, we found ourselves with little cash on hand and did not have tens of thousands of dollars sitting in an account that we could use for earnest money deposits. You may have thought at some point, "If I don't have $10,000 and that is what I need to put into escrow, how can someone like me get started?" As is the case for most people who are successful, I had to think or quit. After research, I learned of an alternative that was called a promissory note.

Since this is such an important discussion point, let's discuss what a promissory note is in a little greater depth. You may not have realized it, but you actually have used them every day of your life. Our dollar serves as a great example of a promissory note. If you look at a dollar bill, it says, "This note is legal tender." A check is a promissory note. A promissory note is legal tender and is accepted as consideration when putting a property under contract. I can create a promissory note for a seller in the amount of $10,000, and it would be legal consideration for that contract. For example, consider if a buyer's note said:

> *I, John Buyer, hereby agree to pay Joe Seller the sum of $10,000 on or before the date of closing for the property located at 123 Main St., Anytown, Florida.*

How is that different from putting cash in escrow? The note says *on or before the date of closing.* If you do not close due to challenges with the property, it never comes due. It is important to note that if you simply do not perform when your contract obligates you to, you may be liable to the seller for the amount you promised to pay. That is what makes promissory notes a very useful yet overlooked or forgotten option for the mobile home park investor.

Since learning of promissory notes, I have used them many times to get properties under contract. We have even put a $1.25 million deal under contract with no money out of our pocket, just by utilizing this tool. When I started, I didn't have $10,000 or $20,000 to put into escrow on every property, and now that I do, I choose not to use it. Promissory notes are one alternative that help the seller see we are serious but preserve our cash for business purposes.

Contract Wrap Up

In this chapter, you have learned how to put a property under contract with zero of your own capital. You also learned how to assign a contract in order to generate a profit even if you are starting from nothing. In addition to this, we have covered many relevant steps to the contracting phase, from different types of contingency clauses to promissory notes. If you are willing to utilize the tools provided in this chapter, you are well on your way to making trailer cash!

Chapter 8

A Walk in the Park

"You are within 200 feet of your destination," the female voice on the GPS announced. After a short flight to Texas and an hour's drive, Ryan and I pulled our rental car into a mobile home park. I love road trips and the thrill of the hunt. So far, this park fit all of our criteria. I spoke with the owner on the phone several times, a sweet lady who sent photos of her park and invited us out for a visit. It looked well-kept and all the numbers looked good. The market was strong, and the park performance was stabilized. If the numbers were accurate, this was going to be a great deal. I kept my excitement in check and reminded myself that, in the end, the numbers make our final decision for us.

I didn't have to keep my excitement in check for very long. The minute we pulled into the park's pebble driveway, I noticed the sign welcoming us to Sunnyville Mobile Home Park was covered in graffiti.

"Okay, that's an easy fix," I said to Ryan. "Not what the photos looked like at all, but—"

I had just caught sight of the roads and the condition of the park—it had seen better days. At least one unit looked so weather-worn it appeared to be sagging under the weight of the sun. Still, I thought of the lovely photos the owner had sent me within the last few weeks. *How old were those photos?*

The thought had just occurred to me that maybe we had entered the wrong address into the GPS when I noticed an elderly lady coming out of her home, waving us to park right in front of her little turquoise trailer. It was the correct park. She greeted us graciously and showed us around her park like a true old Southern belle. She also brought us into her home to show us her well-kept rent rolls and the active leases for all the lots. The numbers seemed to be there, based on what they were providing to us, but something wasn't right. Just as the owner continued to give me the overview of the property, I continued building a list of concerns based on items I quickly noticed.

Rather than spend my time listening to the owner's pitch on how wonderful the property was, I did what I always do and that is let the facts speak for themselves. As I always say, "People may lie, but numbers don't."

As she had just finished showing me the updated rent rolls, I immediately sought to confirm what she had shown. You have to remember, I am buying this property to earn a profit, so not checking each number for accuracy invites risk into the likelihood that I will be profitable. I was already at the property, so I figured I would go on a little door-knocking campaign. I quickly excused myself from the meeting with the owner and the manager and went out into the park.

After a quick tour of the property, it was clear there were occupancy issues, electrical issues, and that the property was in a state of disrepair. Once again, nothing like the photos that had been sent in. Some of the issues could be quickly remedied, but others were going to take a significant amount of time and budget to complete. On our round of the property, it was fairly easy to see that several of these homes were abandoned, despite the rent rolls saying otherwise. The neighbors confirmed this by telling us how long the homes had been vacant.

When we went back to discuss the deal with the owner, the current park manager was there too. I calmly went over all her information to give her the chance to 'fess up. But they both simply nodded "yes, yes, yes" to everything. It became obvious they were in cahoots. The seller had even gone so far as to fabricate the leases that did not exist, and now she was lying right through her dentures.

You should have seen the look on her face when we let her know we knew they were empty. And the photos of the park she sent me? They were over two years old. It was clear the owner knew the property needed to be performing at a higher level to justify the purchase price. Instead of creating real value through some improvements to the property over the years, she painted a picture of the property that would have made Enron proud. Just like every transaction we enter into, we will pay a fair price for actuals, not pro forma, and certainly not based on made-up numbers from the land of Oz.

Due to the number of discrepancies with the park and its records, we could only wonder what else was false. What other issues lay ahead? Due to all of the issues identified with the park, we walked. Without wasting one more minute, we continued our search for good deals.

One of our basic business principles is to buy properties that are performing. We don't mind improving a property and maximizing the income on an asset that is already performing, but we certainly don't want to be sucking wind financially when our intent was to purchase a cash-flowing asset. That is a financial drain on a monthly basis.

What is due diligence? Again, it's the process of making sure you are buying what you think you are buying. For us, it begins with a 52-point checklist. It's sleuthing. It's a scavenger hunt and a cross-examination. You're Sherlock in search of the facts.

To perform due diligence, observe the park at night to check out the activity level, good and bad. If half the lights are out and no cars are in the driveway, the units are likely vacant. Ask around the community. Knock on doors. Check out public records at the local city hall. Run market comparisons with nearby parks to compare occupancy numbers, rental rates, conditions of neighboring properties, and the like. If nearby parks claim significantly different numbers, mainly as it pertains to occupancy and rental rates, that's a hot clue that something is amiss. Question the owner about these differences. For example, if you are looking at a property that is 80 percent occupied and every other mobile home park in town is at 95 percent, there is most likely an opportunity there. However, if you are on the only property in town that seems to be occupied properly, that could be a sign of a local economic situation you need to look into.

As the prospective buyer, you have every right to be asking questions. In fact, it is nobody's job but yours to do so. A thorough verification of the details specified in your contract may be the most important step in MHP investing. It keeps you out of bad deals. Missing information, or misinformation, can also be what you need to make a good deal even better. Due diligence means collecting the facts and reading between the lines. Small details can make a big difference. I recently read that the former coach of the Indiana Hoosiers basketball team, Bobby Knight, was asked in an interview on *60 Minutes*, "What does it take to be a team that's continually in the top rankings and continually winning? It must certainly take the will to win."

Due diligence means collecting the facts and reading between the lines. Small details can make a big difference.

Knight replied, "It does. It takes the will to win. However, it primarily takes something even more important than that. It takes the will to prepare. It takes the will to go out every day and practice the fundamentals over and over until they become second nature, and then first nature to you."

A Walk in the Park

As a tomboy growing up, I played every sport my brothers did and loved every minute of it. It was rigorous. It was competitive. It was exhausting. It was fun to be part of a team. And at the end of the day, it just felt good, especially to win.

As a businesswoman now, I understand that the desire to win and the work it actually takes to win are two different things. Everyone wants to be a winner in life. But who among us puts in the daily practice? As a real-estate investor, winning means closing on a great deal that performs to your expectations. Every day in my business, my plan is to win. That takes due diligence. Deals fall through, like the one in Texas. You get up and face the next opportunity as a potential win. And the next. And the next.

Due diligence is a process of repitition—you go through the same steps over and over until you score the next fantastic win for the team. The team is you, your family, and your business. This is how building wealth becomes a habit. Then you show up at the closing table prepared to win. You will have thoroughly evaluated the property you're about to purchase, and you are confident it will perform at the level you expect. It's your offense and your defense.

Many investors express concern about competition. If you are concerned about competition, you are most likely not performing to the best of your ability. Like any coach would, I encourage new investors to get out there and get going, as worrying about what *might* happen *if* you make a move can be paralyzing. If you know what you're doing, there are numerous opportunities out there. Ryan and I have acquired more real estate in this economic contraction than in the preceding period of economic expansion. It is truly a buyer's market, and it always will be if you gain the tools to enable you to win in this game. Over time, the economy will expand as well as contract. There will always be sellers, and I will always be buying.

The difference between investing without due diligence or making it your priority is the difference between Michael Jordan and George from Seinfeld going to the gym. They both spend time at the gym, but only one is walking out with the benefit he was looking for.

Okay, you get the point. Preparation for success in the mobile home park business lies in how thoroughly you complete the due-diligence phase. Why does Warren Buffet get such great and consistent rates of return on his investments compared to the average day trader or Wall Street broker? He implements a conservative approach, and he does his homework. The man with his finger on the pulse of the economy has amassed billions based on a practice of thorough research.

What we do during our due-diligence phase on mobile home parks is no different. It's my job as the buyer to perform the due diligence, and I need the help of the seller to provide some of the information. We meet the owners, see how the park has been maintained, search around for hidden surprises (good or bad), and stay overnight to continue the process of observation and information gathering at night and the next day.

If what we find during the due-diligence process is not exactly as the seller told us up front, I don't take that as a deal breaker. But anything worth noting during due diligence will create a point for renegotiation.

Fact-finding and verification, coupled with leveraging the wrong valuation model, in my opinion, were the biggest missing pieces of the puzzle in the real-estate boom that led to the crash and burn of the housing market in general. If investors knew how to perform cash-flow analysis, they wouldn't be in the trouble they are now. In terms of residential real estate, the overinflated housing market would have, in many cases, appeared far too pricey for a value investor and would have caused you to sit on the sidelines, saving you from the downward spiral that was to follow. I find it quite ironic that now that value has returned to many markets, investors are skittish and are reluctant to buy for fear of losing money. The reason? They do not know how to spot value to begin with and are not prepared with the tools needed to perform a comprehensive due-diligence process.

How can we know that seller is telling the truth when they provide us with information? We can't. In fact, we assume they are fibbing, erring, or lying. We consider it our responsibility to discern the truth. Think of it this way: if a seller lies with the information provided to you and you accept it, are you not the one who is ultimately responsible? I have heard hundreds, if not thousands, of stories from investors all over the globe purporting to be ripped off by the seller, or lender, or appraiser. You know, when you begin to find fault with everyone everywhere, you must remember that the only common denominator is you. I once read a story of a man who had been married thirteen times and was looking for his "dream girl." Get real! What are the odds that he married thirteen women with issues? Statistically, he is the one with the problem!

If you are reading this now and have non-performing assets in your portfolio, do not involve yourself in the blame game. Let me save you some time. Go to the nearest mirror, point at it, and know that you are the person who made the mistake. The failure to learn from past mistakes is the biggest failure of all. That being said, fail forward. Now that you have identified the error, you can improve your approach and prevent it from happening again.

Due-Diligence High Points

You now know the role that due diligence plays in a transaction and its importance in the process of acquiring properties. Let's now discuss some of the high points of this process.

Income and occupancy

Most sellers keep terrible records. Insist on getting copies of rent rolls, bank statements, and other documentation to affirm the property's long-term track record. (By "long-term," we are looking for two years or more.) Then confirm the stated income matches the actual income.

More often than not, owners paint a better picture than you find. In some cases, though, the reality is even better than you expected.

You may find yourself considering a property that fits the bill for the most part but has some occupancy issues caused by management or deferred maintenance. When you identify issues like this, the first question to ask is always, "How much will it cost and how long will it take to remedy?" If the issues you uncover are relatively benign, like the occupancy rate being slightly different than stated, you could simply renegotiate based on the adjusted figures or get creative. You could use an event-driven contract, which we previously discussed, to say, "Closing to take place after the occupancy reaches 90 percent." I would prefer to renegotiate and take on the improvements myself in most cases. I know what needs to be done and can most likely accomplish it faster and more efficiently than the seller. This also gets the seller to a closing, which is ultimately what they want. As always, if the issues are serious and the seller is not willing to work with you to remedy them, you can always cancel the contract, assuming your contract allows you to do so.

> More often than not, owners paint a better picture than you find. In some cases, though, the reality is even better than you expected.

Property and income taxes

When doing your due diligence, you always want to request copies of the seller's tax returns for the past years. More than any other type of real estate, mobile home parks tend to be a cash business.

You will often find sellers having two sets of books. While this is common, I caution you from operating your business in this manner. Just because you can get away with something doesn't make it moral, just, or even legal. Have integrity in all that you do, even if it costs you more money. Due to the "two sets of books issue," the tax returns are not always helpful. Ask anyway. A lot of these due-diligence steps encourage honesty and full disclosure from sellers.

Note: In the mobile home park business, there are often property taxes and personal property taxes due. We knew someone buying a mobile home park who did property tax research on the park but didn't check for tax liens on the homes, and it turned out the seller owed over $30,000 in property taxes on the homes he owned in the park. When the property sold, the new owner was told to bring those back taxes current or lose those homes. It was a huge, unnecessary financial hit. If the buyer had gone that one extra step to do a little research on the personal property taxes, this would have been avoided.

Utilities

Utilities play a big role in profit generation, so this is a very important section that we will cover in full detail. Inexperienced investors would never even think to ask these questions, but you will want to find out:

- Does the mobile home park's water come from the city, a private utility company, a private utility system, or a well?

- Does the waste go to a septic system or city sewers?

Neither of these options necessarily constitute a problem. City water and city sewer, however, are the preferred option. If your mobile home park is on well water and a septic system, it is not a deal breaker. But be aware you are responsible—at your expense—for the well and the septic tanks and any issues that arise. So while it's not a deal breaker, you don't want it to be an unpleasant surprise, either. Budget ahead of time.

Some of the other important questions are:

- Who pays the utility bills—the tenants or the park owner?
- How much are the monthly electrical bills?
- How much are the water bills?
- What amperage are the pads in the park?

Years ago, we bought a well-performing park at a good price, knowing full well that there was only one water meter on the whole property, meaning one bill. All these years, the owner paid everyone's water bill, which was approximately $2,000 per month, assuming it was his cost of doing business! He actually felt really bad about the idea of passing on that expense to the tenants. Can you believe that? I look at it this way. At my home, no one pays for my utilities, so I shouldn't pay for anyone else's.

From the onset, we saw an opportunity to pass the water-usage cost back to the tenants by sub-metering each unit in the park. That's exactly what we did. We installed a separate water meter at every pad. The investment, which we got from a business line of credit, easily paid for itself in a matter of months. This meant that our net income was $24,000 a year higher than it was when we bought it by making this change.

If you are an eco-conscious investor, sub-metering a property has also been found to decrease water consumption by approximately 25 percent. So it is good for your pocketbook and good for the environment.

A Walk in the Park

When we find parks with only one utility meter, we see it as an opportunity to increase our profits. As I have mentioned many times, we only buy performing assets. The property performed the day of closing, but the opportunity to sub-meter after closing allows for a significant value-added opportunity, which can lead to increased profits as well as equity.

A few people moved out as a result of this change, but they were the ones who hadn't paid their rent regularly anyway. Who doesn't have to pay for their water usage? You're not Mr. Bad Guy if you sub-meter the park; you're Mr. Reality Check. On a side note, if you are an eco-conscious investor, sub-metering a property has also been found to decrease water consumption by approximately 25 percent. So it is good for your pocketbook and good for the environment.

As mentioned in chapter 6, we use the following formulas for mobile home park valuation as it pertains to the park paying the utilities versus the tenant paying.

Example 1: The park pays utilities

Purchase price = occupied lots *x* lot rent *x* 60

Example 2: The tenants pay their own utilities

Purchase price = occupied lots *x* lot rent *x* 70

Now, let's look at an example from an actual park:

- Occupied lots: 45
- Lot rent: $250

At purchase, the park paid the utilities:

45 *x* $250 *x* 60 = $675,000

When sub-metered and tenants paid their own utilities:

$$45 \times \$250 \times 70 = \$787{,}500$$

The value difference was $112,500! Now, let's say it costs $750 per meter to sub-meter each unit in the park through the city. I have had investors say, "$750 per unit?! I can do that myself for $150." While that is true, you may be missing some benefits. In most cases, when the local utility provider handles the installation, they will pick up the cost to read the meters, will bill the tenants, and will become responsible for the water and sewer lines up to the home. All this removes you from the utility business completely.

Having the utility company sub-meter the property in this scenario would cost the owner $33,750. Not only does sub-metering increase the value of the property, it also increases the monthly cash flow. In this case, it is a reduction of $2,000 per month in water and sewer expense.

Let's continue with this example in order to show some more numbers. Let's say that through our due diligence we found out this property is about $25 per lot below market value in its monthly lot rent fee. What do the numbers look like after the rental increase, considering the same formula above?

$$45 \text{ lots} \times \$275 \text{ rent} \times 70 = \$866{,}250 \text{ purchase price}$$

In this example, there were two simple opportunities to take advantage of this acquisition:

1. A rental increase
2. Sub-metering the water and sewer

These two actions increased the value approximately $200,000 while also improving the buyer's monthly cash flow. Not bad for two improvements to the park! The key to making this type of profit yours is understanding the business.

Expenses

Tracking expenses—let's just say it's not every park owner's forte. Most owners eat their own expenses because, for the most part, they don't treat the park like a professional business. We expect a 40 percent expense ratio on parks that pay for the utilities and 30 percent on parks that do not. Any significant variance from that will get our attention.

Find out what the seller spends, if anything, for advertising; bank charges; licenses and permits; utilities; mowing and landscaping; maintenance, labor, and supplies; and management. Waste management is one of the nickel-and-dime expenses that really adds up. It may not sound like a big deal, but some of these parks cost you $500 a month for trash pickup. That's $6,000 a year that you don't want to overlook. It's ideal if the garbage service is handled within the water and sewer bill and paid for by the tenant.

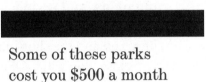

Some of these parks cost you $500 a month for trash pickup. That's $6,000 a year you don't want to overlook.

Documents

Get all the documents you need from a seller prior to closing. Once they get their money, they are eager to move on.

- **Titles to homes**. You need these, and you need to ask for them. Sellers may not have all the titles to the homes you may be acquiring. In that case, be sure to get a bill of sale for each home.

- **Photos of the park**. Photos help you to see the layout of the park, age of the homes, conditions of the roads, landscaping, quality of signage, and so on. Even Google Earth or Microsoft Live's aerial view is fun to use when you're negotiating over the phone: "Oh, do you mean the third unit down from the first row?" This will not give you the detail of the pictures you are asking for, but it is a great tool when negotiating over the phone and viewing the area in general.

- **Diagrams of underground infrastructure, plumbing, and wiring**. It's a real nightmare when there's a problem and nobody knows where the lines run and the shut-offs are. Ask for these before you close. You will be glad you did when there is an issue.

- **Rental application, lease, and copies of current leases**. You will likely update the lease agreement, but keep the originals on file because when you buy a property, you have to honor the existing leases until they expire.

- **Home condition reports**. If you are acquiring any mobile homes with your purchase, be sure to evaluate each home so that you will be able to budget appropriately for any unforeseen expenses. If the issues have a significant enough cost to them, this can be used when renegotiating.

- **List of major appliances and park equipment**. We ask for everything that's used in the operations of the mobile home park, such as mowers, weed eaters, any extra air conditioners, and the like. If you don't ask, you don't get. Photos and video are as much for psychological leverage as for physical documentation.

- **Names and numbers of service providers**. This "minor detail" makes the ownership transition much smoother. You will want to have the service transition lined up for closing date. It is smart to have all these contacts and numbers lined up before closing—including the phone company, advertising, electric and water companies, etc.

- **Land survey**. You own what a piece of paper says you own, so you'd better make sure that piece of paper is accurate. Once we discovered that a park we were buying had three addresses because it was three separate parcels of land. Had we not clarified all three addresses with the legal descriptions in the contract, we would have only owned one-third of what we thought we owned!

A Valuable Perspective for Due Diligence

I have learned over the years that some investors fall in love with the idea of owning a property so much that they compromise the quality of their research to get to the goal of ownership. The problem is, owning a property that is not profitable is ownership that I would not want to be a part of. This isn't a romance novel. This is investing. Unless you are Elton John, leave the rose-colored glasses at home.

When you first get a lead on a prospective property, you must look at the property almost from a view of non-interest. Through the due-diligence process, I let the facts convince me that I should own it rather than deciding early on based solely on emotion.

Deal Breakers—Know When to Run

Here are some deal breakers to watch out for. Cancel the transaction under the following circumstances.

Failed phase one environmental review

If a park fails a phase one environmental review, cut your losses and cancel the contract. It probably means the location was formerly a dumping site or presents some sort of chemical contamination risk. The test costs two to three thousand dollars, but it can save you a lot of money down the line. There are situations that warrant you walk away from a deal, and this is one that you would run from. From time to time, I am asked if I would follow up with a phase two or a phase three study. The answer is no. There are plenty of deals out there, so I would move on at this point.

Declining market

If you're in a location where jobs are disappearing and plants are shutting down, there's no economic viability for owning the park. It's not even worth the small amount they are probably asking if there is no demand for housing or there's a potential for declining demand in the future.

Know When the Deal Is Done

Warning: don't stay in the due-diligence phase too long. Move through the process quickly. The goal is to buy a good deal with a monthly cash flow. However, this doesn't mean that every discrepancy you come across in the due-diligence phase is a deal breaker. Consider the issue and what it means to the value and the performance of the property. Sometimes there are issues that are not deal breakers. Keep track of these items and their effect on the deal. You will use this if it is necessary to renegotiate the deal.

Once you have completed your due diligence to your satisfaction and reviewed the impact of your findings toward the performance of the property, you may want to sit down with the seller to renegotiate. This is where your professionalism wins the day. The more calm and non-confrontational you are, the more professional the seller will be with you in return. Go through your list point by point, and if an agreement is reached, reflect that agreement through an addendum to the original contract.

Now that you have sealed the deal, you will need to implement management systems (which we will discuss in a future chapter) to improve on the property's performance and to maximize its profits.

I grew up in the eighties. I remember when we worried about whether we could trust the Russians or not. President Ronald Reagan had a policy that he said was actually a Russian maxim: "Trust but verify." In fact, he repeated this phrase in a meeting in Russia with Mikhail Gorbachev. Those present at the meeting said,

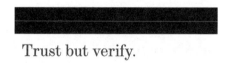

Trust but verify.

"You repeat that at every meeting." President Reagan laughed with the audience, then paused, turned to Gorbachev, and said, "I like it." Laughter rippled across the room. This is the approach I take, as well, and you should too.

Chapter 9

Breaking the Bank

If you are like most people, the mere task of obtaining financing for a property seems larger than life and sometimes insurmountable. Don't misunderstand. When I started my business, I was in a similar position with a similar view. As I have grown my business in the face of various uncertainties, these once insurmountable problems have all but faded into the background. You see, most people see access to capital as a problem when, for most people, it is having the knowledge of how to access the capital that is the real culprit.

Let me give you an example. In the first major town nearest to where you currently live, do you think there is $1 million of net worth represented by all the citizens it contains? What about $10 million? What about $1 billion? The answer is yes! So if you have a location that contains a significant capital base, the question isn't, "Where is it?" The question instead becomes, "How do I access it?" or, more importantly, "What do I have that someone with a higher net worth needs?" The answer is obviously not more money, but is typically far more subtle. The answer is competence. People invest in people with competence (or the perception thereof).

Let me ask you a question. What would you think of the real-estate business as a whole if you could simply walk into a banker's office and ask for a loan where you state the details of the property, set the terms of your loan, and it is done in a matter of minutes?

In this chapter, you will learn how this is, in fact, possible and much more.

What a bank wants

In all aspects of a transaction, you must constantly be asking yourself what the person on the other side of the table wants. Understanding the other person and their wants and needs is imperative to accomplishing anything in life. You must see through their eyes.

A bank operates much like you would if you were them. To understand risk is to understand a bank. A bank, for obvious reasons, does not want to risk their money when it comes to the activity of lending.

Against the backdrop of risk, then, let's discuss the mobile home park industry as a whole. Historically, mobile home parks have enjoyed a relatively lower default rate compared to other types of commercial real estate. This, coupled with the high demand, low vacancy, and restricted supply (due to permitting challenges), the case for investing in mobile home parks has actually become more attractive over this contracted economic period.

"But what if I don't earn enough income to qualify for a loan?" This is a question I get at almost every speaking engagement. While it's a good question, it is rooted in the residential market. You must know, the residential market and the commercial market are two separate markets and are not to be confused.

Let me give you an example. When you purchase a house in the residential market, a lender will typically ask for your wage history to make sure that your income can support the loan. Many people I meet have purchased a single-family house to live in and think that is investing. What I do is so different. When you purchase a single-family residence, many times there isn't any income being brought in each month, so your income is required in order to qualify for the loan.

This is where commercial real estate in general is much different. When purchasing a mobile home park, the income of greatest interest to the lender is the income from the mobile home park, since that is what will be used to pay the lender each month. The lender is far less worried about you and far more interested in the income being produced by the asset. It's interesting to note that in many cases, it can be easier to finance a thirty-unit mobile home park than a single-family house!

If you have already attempted to purchase a mobile home park, this may help explain why the financing process was different than you may have expected. When a lender looks at a mobile home park, they only care about one source of income: the income from the lots. If the mobile home park rents out a lot for $250 but rents the mobile home with the lot for $495, the bank is only going to recognize the $250. People ask me about this all the time. If a mobile home is owned by the park and the park owner is renting out the home and the lot for $495, why doesn't the lender accept the full $495 as the income for that lot? The answer is because the lender is only interested in the income derived from real property, not the personal property. A mobile home is considered personal property, much like your car or a boat. Lenders do not prefer to lend on mobile homes because they represent increased expenses, are depreciating assets, and are relatively mobile. Think about it in light of these risks:

- **Increased expenses.** The personal property brings a significant amount of variable expense with it in the way of material costs, management, maintenance, turnover, etc. Lenders are looking for the least amount of risk, and dirt that doesn't need a new A/C, a new roof, or a new toilet is certainly a lot less risk than lending against the homes with all of these potential problems and more.

- **Inconsistency in income.** The average tenancy for a mobile home is ten months, while the average occupancy for a mobile home lot is years.

- **Homeowner-occupied communities.** Have you driven through a neighborhood lately with a lot of "For Rent" signs in it? Were the homes kept up? How were the yards? Most likely, the neighborhood was run down and not nearly as well taken care of as a homeowner-occupied neighborhood where the people living in their homes actually care about their homes and take care of them. There is no difference in a mobile home park. Pride of ownership exists in the same way. The overall quality of a community will impact the consistency of the income and the overall property value, and the banks understand this. They prefer to lend on mobile home parks with less than 25 percent of the lots having homes that are owned by the park.

Due to these reasons, the lender will include only the lot rental income and the expenses associated with the lot rent when evaluating a park.

Let me give you an example to make sure you are following me here.

- Sunshine State Mobile Home Park
- 50 lots with 12 park-owned homes
- Lot rent: $250
- Home rental with lot: $495
- Occupancy: 100%
- Gross income, according to the seller: ($250 x 38) + ($495 x 12) = $15,440
- Gross income, according to the bank: ($250 x 50) = $12,500

Without going into this example further, note that lenders are only interested in the income derived from the land, and if you are using conventional financing, this is how it works.

Seller financing

There is always a way to structure a deal that can be successful if both parties are willing to be creative. That's called creative financing. Creative financing includes a variety of options, but seller financing offers the greatest benefits and flexibility for both buyer and seller. You and the seller design the deal yourselves.

Before we start discussing seller financing and providing examples, it is important to clarify what seller financing is. Seller financing is basically when the person selling the property acts as the lender on the property rather than having the buyer acquire a loan from a third-party banker. For example, Benjamin Jones may have a property he wants to sell and I want to buy. Instead of acquiring a loan from Wells Fargo, the seller might agree to finance the property directly to me. Instead of making my payments to Wells Fargo, I am making my payments to the "Bank of Benjamin Jones." Seller financing is a commonly-used financing instrument in commercial property and is an excellent example of creative financing. In 2008 and 2009 alone, 56 percent of commercial deals that were closed had a seller-financing component.

Let me give you an example that appeared unfortunate at first, but later made the deal beneficial for everyone because of this approach.

One of our stay-at-home moms cold-called an older gentleman from Tennessee named Bubba. When she asked if he was interested in selling his property, he very enthusiastically said, "Why, yes, I am." After he answered her questions from our Mobile Home Park Quick Evaluation Sheet, she turned the lead over to me and I called Bubba right away. I know, it sounds like I made up that stereotypical name, but that is actually what he went by, and yes, I was expecting an interesting character on the other line. But this gentleman was kind and well spoken and more concerned for his family than himself. In the course of talking on the phone, he revealed the full story.

Bubba had happily owned the park for twenty years, but he was now seventy-eight and getting too old to run it. Doctors had recently found a tumor above his brain. He wanted to pass on a legacy to his son and then his grandson, but there was a catch. His son had a drug problem, and the seller did not want his son to inherit the park because he was afraid he'd run it into the ground. Neither did he want to leave his son a lump sum of cash because he would blow through all the money and have nothing to leave his grandson. He felt his options were to leave the park to his son, who would likely destroy the park, or leave him with a lump sum of cash that would only feed his addiction. Bubba wanted to get out from under it but felt stuck between a rock and a hard place.

After listening to his circumstances, it was clear that seller financing would be a good option for him. It would allow him to get out of the day-to-day management but still benefit from an income stream. He would need money for medical bills and a steady income for his surviving family. This would also eliminate the problems he had determined if he left the property to his son.

In the course of our conversation, I asked, "How much would you like to sell the park for?" (Remember it's good negotiation practice to get the seller to throw out the first number.)

He immediately responded, having already thought about it, "$330,000." Based on the information from our Mobile Home Park Quick Evaluation Sheet, we knew this was a phenomenal asking price. We immediately faxed over the offer without even thinking twice. We designed a unique deal that would work for the seller, as well as for us.

We purchased the land and the park-owned homes that would come with the park separately. We acquired private financing and seller financiing on this deal so Bubba could receive a lump sum of money upfront for himself and his wife. He held the balance of the note of what was due in a mortgage note against the property. This allowed him to earn a steady income stream.

By financing the property, Bubba could receive monthly income and could control the income stream his son received monthly in the event of his death. Brilliant! The thing that made this deal even better is that we only had to put down $18,000 on the deal in combination financing.

In short, we acquired the park on a seller-financed note with an extremely low amount down. We structured a deal that meted out the money to him for the sale of his property and provided for his family's long-term security, and everybody benefited, even our stay-at-home mom who made the initial cold call for us.

The flexibility to do a combination loan is completely unique to MHPs. As an investor, you can purchase the land and the homes separately and split them into two separate loans. You can literally design your deals to suit each circumstance. Very few investors are even aware of this special attribute of MHP investments.

Now we own a fifty-six-unit mobile home community in a major city. At $330,000 and $5,800 per lot, that park has been an income generator from day one. You can value parks in several different ways, and that park was a great deal no matter how you looked at it. Now that it's worth double that, we are realizing the potential we initially saw. That was one of those "right time, right place, right price" scenarios. We just called Bubba recently to stay in touch, and he's doing well despite some continuing medical problems. He expressed his relief over not having to manage the park anymore, day in and day out, but he was especially glad he no longer needed to worry about his family's future.

Another interesting twist to this is the opportunity to pay off seller-held notes at a reduced amount. I can share two examples, among many, where this happened. The first example is the rest of Bubba's mobile home park story.

I spoke to Bubba recently, and he's continuing to deal with medical problems. He asked us if we would be willing to refinance and pay him off. If so, he would be willing to take significantly less than what was due to him. We agreed to refinance. This benefitted him by allowing him to gain access to cash that he did not originally need. We benefittted by getting a significant discount on what was owed.

Another example of how seller-financing notes can be an opportunity down the road comes from another park we own in Texas. That particular MHP was purchased for $950,000 with two seller-held notes. We put $100,000 down. One seller financed a $550,000 note, and the other financed a $300,000 note. We purchased this park several years ago. The health of both sellers deteriorated as they grew older. One of the sellers recently passed away, but prior to her death, she married a gentleman and made him the beneficiary of her $300,000 note. The gentleman she married thought he had hit the lottery. As oftentimes happens, the individuals that receive an inheritance want to spend it as soon as possible. Having talked to the beneficiary of this note, we knew that was the case for him. Ryan and I took a look at the situation and considered some different options with the seller for the $550,000 note and the surviving heir for the $300,00 note. After talking with them and understanding their needs, we offered them payoff amounts. The gentleman who inherited the $300,000 note accepted a $108,000 offer. The other seller accepted $450,000 for the $550,000 note. Due to the changing circumstances and needs of the sellers, we were able to see an opportunity and negotiate a reduction in principal of $292,000, just by asking and negotiating. That was a nice payday.

Creative financing can literally be as easy as that. From a list of parks in one particular state, our researcher happened to dial Bubba's number when that gentleman needed it the most. She was also compensated very nicely in exchange for her work in finding the property. She essentially made $30,000 for making a phone call! In the end, our creative financing was a blessing to Bubba who wanted to sell it, it's been a valuable cash-flowing asset to our company, and it's benefited our researcher. *That* is what we mean by mutual respect and mutual benefit.

I was always taught, "Treat others the way you want to be treated. And do the right thing even when no one is watching." Remember that on the day you go into a park owner's office or home with the intention of creating mutual respect and mutual benefit, your attitude about helping them while helping yourself will come across clearly. Your approach to the conversation with the seller can cause that relationship to change from something potentially adversarial to a real business partnership. It also makes this part of the business far more fun and effective.

The Right Time Is Now

Some people say, "It's not a good time to invest in an unstable real-estate market. There are too many loan restrictions and requirements for getting a loan right now." At this point in our business, we have invested through economic expansion and contraction, boom and bust, and affordable housing is needed more today than ever. But, more importantly, it is needed in every economy.

Treat others the way you want to be treated. And do the right thing even when no one is watching.

That being said, I have also heard every excuse under the sun for why people fail to take action. Don't get me wrong, there are always challenges, but there are challenges in everything. That's life, but that also is what makes life fun and what gives me a sense of accomplishment. I work out every morning in Orlando with the leading sports performance group in town so that I can be challenged. I can tell a distinct difference in my day from having overcome physical challenges in the morning. Overcoming challenges allows you to gain a sense of satisfaction and only allows you to accomplish more in the future.

Ironically, we have heard people recently say that the credit crunch has made investing in real estate harder. We have found the opposite to be true. Investing in low-income housing makes the best sense because it works in all economies. Sellers want to sell, but they can't sell because buyers cannot get a bank loan. Seller financing bridges that gap. The credit crunch has actually created an increased incentive for seller financing and is an excellent time to be buying!

You, the buyer, benefit during an economic contraction because the sellers are motivated to work with the buyers that are available. Unlike dealing with a huge bank or financial institution, the buyer has the ability to explain his or her situation. This type of lending is much more relational versus the traditional banking approach where you're told, "Fill out the application and we'll let you know."

An investor friend of mine who recently declared bankruptcy explained to a seller that his financial state was due to a recent divorce. In this case, the park owner went for the deal anyway because he had known hard times himself and could relate to the person buying his property. Personally, I think people's behavior should count for something. I don't think a person's financial credibility can be completely defined by a credit report. Plenty of folks have had serious medical issues that were totally unforeseeable. They lost everything and their credit is in the toilet, yet they didn't do anything wrong. They were not untrustworthy, just unprepared, and life caught them off guard. Banks can be unreasonably prohibitive sometimes, even in a reasonable scenario. You could be a creditworthy borrower but default on one medical bill and be denied a loan. Just so you know, you can apply seller financing in all areas of real estate, as well as other areas of investment.

Negotiating for the Best Deal

You have a lot of open territory in which to trade and negotiate, particularly with seller financing. It's cliché, but true—everything is negotiable, especially in MHP investments. Here are the numbers you will need to understand to negotiate your best deal possible:

- Purchase price
- Interest rate
- Payback period
- First payment date
- Interest type (or no interest)

In most cases, I understand these numbers and how they impact the seller better than they do. Some of these sellers have been collecting rent in cash for years and their accounting system is often a manila envelope on the front seat of their truck. My approach is to do my homework and come prepared. I understand the park's value based on the cash-flow analysis. So

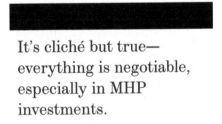

It's cliché but true—everything is negotiable, especially in MHP investments.

if an owner asks for more than the property is really worth, rather than argue, I gently prod him to justify why he thinks it's worth that. I prefer to understand where the owner is coming from. If he cannot justify the asking price, it is best he realizes for himself that the price is not reasonable than for me to tell him. If he holds his ground, I simply explain why the value of the property is different than he anticipated. I am sure to have the conversation discussing the value of their property based on the numbers.

Let's Make a Deal: Benefits of Seller Financing for the Seller

In your initial discussions with the seller regarding price, you will want to present the concept of seller financing. Your ability to negotiate this successfully is going to be strongly tied to your ability to discuss this option and its virtues for the sellers.

We present three offers at the same time, one being conventional. I'll talk about those three offers in a moment. First, I want to explain how we look at the deal.

Let's say we buy a hot property for half a million dollars and the owners get that $500,000 in one shot. Woohoo! They are excited for about two seconds. Then the government comes along and wants to take a nice chunk of that money for themselves in capital-gains tax. Then, after paying the agent or lawyer a percentage, the owner sees that his money is quickly getting chipped away and socks the rest into a bank account—but not before buying that condo or giving a chunk to his kids' college funds. The lump sum just got quite a bit smaller. Maybe the seller's retirement fund grows at a rate above the rate of inflation, if he's lucky. If not, the value of the money deflates in a low-interest bank account.

Suddenly, the seller's "big payday" scenario doesn't sound so sweet. He ends up with a couple assets, a boat or maybe a Harley that sits in the driveway depreciating, along with his or her nest egg. Besides that, what does he have to show for the sale? Has his lifestyle improved? Have his long-term concerns and worries disappeared? No, because the seller still doesn't have a regular steady income scheduled to support him and his family for the next twenty to thirty years—which we include in the term of the seller-financed loan we then propose.

We negotiate the finer points from there, such as how much money will we put up front for the down payment and how long the amortization schedule will be. What are the owners' current circumstances versus their dreams? I always start by asking a lot of questions, a few are:

- Why are they interested in selling?
- What are they going to do with the money when they receive it?

If the owners mention, "We are sure looking forward to moving to Florida. Plan to buy a boat too," for example, that tells me how much they would need for a down payment. If they just say, "Man, we are just tired of the management headaches," I figure they are just hoping for a steady income into their golden years. A consistent income stream is always an intriguing alternative for any seller under any circumstances.

The Three-Offer-Option Surprise

We usually introduce the idea of seller financing during our negotiations and develop it further when we present our offers. When it's time for financing, we present the owners with at least three payment options. This is such a great negotiating technique because it removes the tit-for-tat atmosphere. I love to hear sellers' responses when they realize it's a workable, good deal for us all. They recognize a win-win when they see it. From the position of trying to get the sellers what they want—and oftentimes even more—we end up working together rather than at cross-purposes.

Sellers appreciate options, as it gives them freedom to choose. Each offer specifies a different amount down, depending on what their needs are, plus monthly payments with differing interest rates and terms. This is our strategy, and it works. Others we have taught have used it successfully as well. In the end, it makes the negotiation process a bit more like teamwork with both parties working toward a workable solution for the buyers and the sellers.

Other types of offers may include variations in price or interest rate, an amortization (payback) schedule, or conventional financing.

Two brothers who came to a training we did about four to five years ago wanted to go into the business with their parents. The boys, in their twenties, came up to us during the course of the weekend and said, "You know, our mother and father have both been in corporate jobs their whole lives. We've watched them work very hard for years, and they aren't nearly close to where they thought they would be in retirement. Now we're looking at our own futures going, 'We don't want to do that. We want an investment that will take us a lot further and do it in a shorter amount of time.'" They also wanted to help their parents by providing resources to assist them in their retirement years.

We had the opportunity to assist these brothers in the process of acquiring their first mobile home park. When they hit on a strong, performing park in Georgia, they called us and we drew up three separate offers.

So let's look at this example. There are a few different approaches in this multi-offer strategy, and I'd like to demonstrate the logic behind it. For example, when this family found a park in Georgia they were interested in purchasing, we helped them run the numbers and put together three offers.

1. The first offer contained the lowest price, the highest interest rate, and the longest amortization schedule (thirty years). The lower price builds in equity and value for the buyers upon sale; the higher interest rate allows for the sellers to make more on a monthly basis; the thirty-year amortization gives the borrowers the flexibility to hold the note long-term or the ability to refinance without an impending deadline.

2. The second offer had a higher offer price than the first offer, a lower interest rate, and a balloon payment of eight years. This offer gives the seller a little bit more on the sale price but less on the interest rate, therefore lowering the relative payment. This offer also requires that the sellers are paid off sooner. The seller's points of interest are the higher price and the faster payback period. The seller does take a reduction on the interest rate and, consequently, the payment, but that's the give-and-take of this offer.

3. The final offer provided for the highest asking price with a low interest rate and a ten-year balloon payment. This offer also provided that half the payments would go directly to principal reduction. This offer price was the highest and a little higher than the buyers wanted to pay. However, the sellers were emotionally attached to the sale price but a lot less focused on the interest rate and amortization schedule.

The desire was to purchase this property and come up with terms that would be suitable for both sides. You may be thinking, *Why would a seller ever agree to a 30-year amortization loan with a balloon in ten years or after 120 payments and agree to accept 60 of those payments as directly paying down the principal?* The real answer is that it doesn't matter why. If you can identify terms that are attractive to the seller and to you, proceed.

For a little more insight on this particular deal, the sellers, wanting the highest offer price, accepted the third offer because they were dead-set on being able to say their property sold for a specific dollar amount. As a buyer, we ran the numbers from our perspective. The seller would have made more if he would have accepted the first offer with a lower asking price and a more traditional payback schedule. But the park owner went for option three. The family put down $50,000, and the property is bringing in $10,000–$11,000 every month. We would have been happy with any of the offers being accepted. If this particular offer made the seller happy, it made us happy.

In case you are intimidated by this idea of negotiating your own deal and are wondering, "Can't I get someone to do that for me?" the answer is, of course you can—if you don't mind giving them up to 10 percent of your profit. They are called real-estate agents. If you would like to do that, I am sure they would appreciate it. However, I assure you, you don't have to have them. It doesn't mean they are not helpful, but you do not have to have an agent to negotiate the best deal. You will be better at negotiating your own deal than someone who doesn't understand what you are trying to create or why they are negotiating the deal for you. If you understand what you are doing and the numbers of the deal, you will be the best person for negotiating your own deal.

Real-estate agents who are hungry for your business can certainly be trained and can be helpful to you in the business. This is not to say you will not come across some skilled agents out there, but you should know your business better than anyone else and not rely on someone else to get you a good deal. At the end of the day I always think to myself, *If someone could earn the types of returns we do, they would not be focused on brokering deals for me; they would be running their own business.*

If you presume that negotiating requires that you "screw the other guy," then it is understandable why you my be squeamish about it. On the contrary, we are in the business of making park owners rich and happy by negotiating for our mutual benefit.

I get this question a lot from new MHP investors: "What if the seller says no?" They're afraid to get rejected. To this, I say, "Make it your goal to get twenty no's." This will not happen, and by not getting those twenty no's, you will get what you want—a good deal. The reality is that you will not get what you want every single time.

Get over it. Of course you will get some no-thank-you's. Move on to the next opportunity.

I love to see a seller's face light up when they realize they are going to make approximately $70,000 a year from interest income for ten years, and that's about $700,000 they never even asked for. I always negotiate with sellers on seller financing by showing them how much more they will make by providing seller financing rather than by using a conventional loan. Suddenly, we are on the same team.

A significant asset to negotiating is knowledge and confidence. They just need to feel confident that you know what you are doing. And you *will* know what you're doing when you finish this book and begin to apply the principles taught here.

From the moment you get an owner on the phone to the moment you close the deal, it will serve you to create a collaborative relationship with them and maintain it throughout your negotiations. Know where the seller is coming from, but remember where you want to go.

One time, we had a seller offer to sell us a property and agreed to seller financing. The only problem holding up the deal was the deciding party in the family could not come to an agreement on what terms would be suitable for them. In the end, we canceled the contract because we were not able to come to an agreement with what would be suitable for them. We walked, but on good terms. A week later, we sent them a letter, generally saying:

Know where the seller is coming from, but remember where you want to go.

Thank you for taking the time to consider our offer. We would be happy to try again at a later date. We sincerely hope you get what you are looking for and wish you all the best.

A year later, they called us back and accepted the terms we originally offered. We got a performing asset with a lower than average down payment and a better interest rate than any bank would ever offer. The closing costs on the deal were around $1,400, whereas a conventional deal would have required $20,000–$30,000 on this particular deal. The sellers got cash up front to get out of ownership (which was their primary desire), plus an ongoing revenue stream that would have otherwise gone to a bank. It is the kind of win-win situation we always shoot for. It happened because we set up that relationship of trust. This is the benefit of treating others with respect.

Don't presume negotiations have to be antagonistic. Successful negotiating has everything to do with being real and being honest.

> Don't presume negotiations have to be antagonistic. Successful negotiating has everything to do with being real and being honest. If you really want to make a lot of money, the big secret is to treat other people with respect.

If you really want to make a lot of money, the big secret is to treat other people with respect.

Whether you get seller or bank financing, or some other means of financing, make sure that you are prepared to manage the property properly. Due diligence will make you wealthy, and management will keep you that way.

Chapter 10

Manage Your Properties, Master Your Life

At this point, we have talked about finding properties, negotiating, contracting, financing, and due diligence. All of these points are hugely important, but none is as important as management. At the end of the day, you can find a property that makes $10,000 per month of net income, but if you cannot manage it, you will never realize the potential you initially saw.

As you create your management strategy, you will need to create many systems that cover your managers, maintenance staff, residents, vendors, and more. In this chapter, we will discuss many of the systems that we have created over the years that have not only saved us countless hours but have made us big money.

Know Your Options

When you acquire a property, you have many different options in terms of your management strategy. Some investors assume they can save a ton of money by managing the property themselves, while most seek to hire a third-party company to handle the management for them. But managing the property yourself will quickly become a headache. The reality is, when you manage the property yourself, with all that entails, and handle the upkeep and maintenance, two things happen:

1. Your time is completely consumed doing things that pay a low hourly wage (if you even cut yourself a check).

2. As an investor, you want to grow your portfolio and build out your investments. If your head is stuck too far into the management sand, you won't have time to focus on the higher-level, higher-value portion of improving and expanding your business.

Of course, building a good management system is necessary. Some people go out and hire a management company to help them. We've been down that road, but we've not encountered a management company yet that can do the job well. If there was, I'd tell you because it would relieve the majority of what I do each week. The best alternative is to have an onsite manager that is not you but is managed by you.

The misperception that managing is a nightmare comes from the fact that many mobile home park owners live, eat, and sleep their job, some for thirty-plus years. Very few ever describe it as a sweet gig. Parks run by owners typically do well because no one cares more about performance than they do. But at the end of the day, how much is the property really making? If it is smaller property and only nets about $3,000 a month, that is not a tremendous reward for all of the effort required of you, the owner, to manage the property full-time. For an employee, it's a different story.

Being your own onsite property manager does *not* save you money, and it costs you too much of your valuable time, which is better spent drumming up the next line of profitable deals. But if you hire a big-name "reliable and professional" property management company to do the work for you, you will typically find they do not care as much as you do, and the result will be lower performance and a reduced profit due to their added expense and management style. Neither option is ideal, so we created a third option—managing the manager.

A friend of ours likes to say, "Accountants live in the past. Managers live in the present. Leaders live in the future." As the leader of your business, having good managers and accountants in place frees you up to dream big. So, let the accountants count your income, let your managers manage, and let yourself focus on the oversight of the current properties as well as the acquisition of future income-producing communities.

You will cultivate your own kind of manager instead; then put a workable, semi-automated system into place to oversee their work so they can achieve your performance objectives. Eventually, when you own enough property and it becomes justified, you can hire a midlevel manager to oversee your multiple properties and park managers. With modern technology, the majority of this can be done remotely.

Others may stress, "But nobody can manage the property better than you, the owner, because anyone you hire won't care as much." While that may be true in some cases, it does not have to be true in all cases. The question should be, "How do I make them care about park quality as much as I do?" The easy answer to that comes from providing incentives. Offer your park manager cash benefits and financial rewards for a job well done. These are fun. I'll show you how they work. But first, I want to make a stronger case here, because I know some of you are still telling yourself, "I think I could still do it to save money." That's the little voice that still thinks like an employee.

> Let the accountants count your income, let your managers manage, and let yourself focus on the oversight of the current properties as well as the acquisition of future income-producing communities.

Get ready to think like a leader, like an investor/owner, and like a future real-estate mogul.

Managing Yourself—Working Hard, Not Smart

There is no point in making a small fortune if you are burning yourself out and not enjoying life in the process. So, believe it or not, we have fun with property management.

Park owners who become managers end up paying themselves probably less than $8 an hour. You may as well be working at the local convenience store because at least you could get discounted hotdogs and sodas. Also, it's implausible unless you buy where you live or move into a mobile home onsite. You want to run the company, not the store. Would you rather be the manager of the McDonald's or own the McDonald's? A lot of people buy franchise businesses to buy themselves a job, and they work their tails off for a moderate income after plunking down six figures for the rights to do so. If I'm going to work that hard, I want the full reward for my effort.

Even if you manage a ten-unit complex perfectly, how many units do you end up with at the end of the day? Ten units. People I talk to who own and manage their own properties are, in their minds, constantly stuck, saying they don't know how they can grow anymore because what they have is driving them nuts. If you are doing everything yourself, it's hard to grow beyond a few units and still be an effective manager without going nuts. Your options are to get stuck at ten to thirty units versus learning how to mobilize a strategy and put systems in place so that you can have an onsite manager at your multifamily properties and enable your company to grow to 200, 400, 1000 units, and beyond like we have done.

But Management Companies Provide Peace of Mind! Or Do They?

Some potential benefits of a management company include the fact that they are QuickBooks savvy. Bookkeeping and tax data come easily. They typically have relationships in the area with maintenance people, hardware stores, appliance dealers, etc. Theoretically, it's the easiest way to handle day-to-day maintenance, collections, and occupancy issues. Theoretically.

It cost us somewhere between $40,000–$50,000 to learn that this isn't always true. Early in our business, we tried one of the most widely recommended companies in the country. The result? Their collection ratio was terrible. Their customer service was an embarrassment. The company overpaid for expenses and materials consistently with our money. So not only were we taking in less than we should have been, but our costs were higher than they should have been. Peace of mind should never come at such a high price.

After our experience, we have met many other property owners that have had similar issues with third-party management companies. Don't assume the property management company knows, or cares, more than you do.

If you choose to go with a property management company, here are a few questions you should ask before hiring them:

1. How many units are they currently managing?

2. How many different landlords are they currently working with?

3. What are their occupancy rates?

4. How long have they been in business?

5. Will they provide at least five names and phone numbers of landlords they represent?

Investigate their reputation by interviewing those individuals. They wouldn't be in business without satisfied clients, but it's easy to pull the wool over the eyes of one or two people. You need a bigger sample to find out if the company would work for you. Talk to four or five of their customers.

That being said, I do not recommend management companies for the simple fact that you get inconsistent results. This inconsistency is usually due to the lack of performance on the management company's part rather than it being the fault of "the property" or "the market." Management companies are notorious for blaming the lack of performance on the property or the market. Given that you did your due diligence properly, you should know the property can perform if run properly.

As I mentioned, Ryan and I learned the blame game of the management companies early on. In the particular situation I was referring to above, every time we questioned something, that manager blamed the market or the property. However, we found out when we fired them and put in our own manager that our income and occupancy both shot up. This, of course, is not to say all management companies are bad, but the point is to bring your attention to a very real challenge that could cost you a lot of money if you don't know better. For those who want to win consistently, not just some of the time, you want to manage your properties internally. Those profit leaks can turn into profit gains.

When we hired our own onsite managers at a few parks ourselves, then hired a management company for the others, the properties managed by the outside company performed at a significantly lower rate time and time again. All the properties run by managers we personally hired kicked their tail. And when we took over the properties the management company managed, their performance rebounded. This made it obvious the issue wasn't market demand. It was just poor management. That was an expensive lesson. As far as we are concerned, the only way to make our mistake a win is if our loss becomes your gain.

Give up on the idea of managing your properties yourself and focus your efforts on managing your managers. Set high expectations and back them up with incentive-based programs.

Cultivate Your Own Manager

The path we highly recommend is for you to handpick, train, and oversee your own manager. You will get good results when you pick the right person, set clear expectations, and follow up. Devote a few minutes every day to speaking with your manager. Your objective is twofold: develop a relationship, and confirm their job is getting done by providing accountability. We train our managers how to make their lives easier by using our efficient management system to produce a higher-performing

Give up on the idea of managing your properties yourself and focus your efforts on managing your managers. Set high expectations and back them up with incentive-based programs.

asset. It's important to train them to value what you value, such as efficiency, reduced expenses, increased revenue, and treating the tenants with respect.

After a while, even when your managers are doing a great job and your properties are performing well, managing your managers will become a full-time job. This is a great problem to have. At this point in our business, we have more than 1,400 units in over eleven states, and we're always looking to invest in more properties. As a result, we utilize midlevel management. I like to talk with our management team every day, but I still work with the individual parks to check in and keep a close eye on individual property performance. We like to run our parks like a mom-and-pop shop and run our business like a Fortune 500 company.

> We like to run our parks like a mom-and-pop shop and run our business like a Fortune 500 company.

Here's another gold nugget. Whether you hire a management company or cultivate your own managers from the area, your results get a boost when you unexpectedly pop into the management office. I recommend quarterly visits, especially early on. Once you've seen performance stabilize for six to twelve months, you don't need to visit as regularly.

Where Can I Find a Good Manager?

Many times you will purchase a mobile home park with management already in place. This can be both good and bad. It all depends on the manager's willingness to implement your systems in the park. For a manager who has been managing a park a specific way for a long period of time, change can create a point of contention. One unspoken rule that we have developed over the years has to do with a manager asking for a raise just after we purchase a property. There have been many times that we have purchased a park and the manager (who was fairly paid) would immediately ask us for a raise. If that is the first question a manager has for us, we go ahead and start looking for the next manager to replace them, as we know that is not a good sign of things to come.

Along with a property, one of our acquaintances recently acquired a property manager who had been there six years. Our friend said, "I'm actually learning a lot from her." Sometimes you acquire a great manager who lives onsite, enjoys the work, and teaches you the ins and outs of the park. One of our parks in Tennessee is run by a lady named Virginia who has managed the park for twenty years. She is competent and genuinely good-natured. Having to learn our new management system challenged her a bit, but she understood the need for improvement in certain areas.

Sometimes you may find managers in place who have been ripping off the previous owner for the last two or three years, or they are simply content to run things "the way they've always been run," so they resist any type of new system you try to implement. They might also work at their own pace, which is never our pace. If they are unable or unwilling to adapt, the need for them to move on is readily apparent and both sides usually recognize it. It will be important to inform the manager and residents that there will be a new manager. We have a standard document that we send out to each resident notifying them of the specific changes and what to expect.

Drawing from the pool of existing tenants is the first step to finding a manager. We send out a letter to introduce ourselves as the new park owners. Here's a summary of a note I may write:

> *(Our company) _____ is acquiring this property in the next couple of weeks. We are looking to hire an onsite property manager. If this is something that you're interested in, or you have property management experience, please fax your resume to _____.*

Schedule in-person interviews to coincide with your due-diligence visit. Sellers are another good source of referrals. They often recommend people in the park who have assisted them or who are involved in the community. One of our most amazing managers is a retired gentleman who is on disability. He's not able to go out to work in a traditional environment, but he enjoys doing the basic maintenance, and people love him at the park. He lives onsite in a very nice triple-wide home. We cover his home ($1,000 per month) plus $500 a month. Usually, we like to pay the manager what is due him or her and ask them to pay for their rent separately. This means we actually pay them with a check instead of bartering or working for their rent. There is a psychological benefit to the manager to see that income coming in. If they don't see a full-sized check, it starts to feel like they are being underpaid because they suddenly forget that the check is smaller because they have fewer bills to pay.

Some people who work locally with mobile home dealers or local property management companies do not typically make a lot of money. They can bring their management experience to your park, and you can offer them incentives like they have never seen. Remember the story I told you about the woman I cold-called in one town's planning department? That's the woman who turned out to have a real-estate agent's license, and she helped us with one of our first great parks. I kept in close touch with her, and we purchased three more parks through her after that. She was able to quit her job at the county, go into business for herself, and hire her friends. She referred us to one of our great park managers. We do not require our managers live onsite, although we prefer that they do.

Good help is not easy to find—it's definitely work. But having an effective management system in place simplifies your investment. Everyone you talk to can become another set of eyes and ears on the ground. Just put the word out and let everyone know what you need.

Interview Questions

As you ask the following questions, look for stability, reliability, initiative, customer service, and willingness to learn new systems.

1. *Do you have any property management experience?*
   It's extremely helpful if they do. The learning curve is going to be a little bit shorter.

2. *Do you have another job?* It's not bad if they do, but it's good to know. If they have been unemployed for the last twelve to twenty-four months, there's probably a reason. Mobile home park management is not a full-time job. However, they do need to be available nights and weekends in case tenants have issues. Most of our managers are in the office for a couple of hours in the morning to do their paperwork, then 4–7 p.m. to be available to tenants.

3. *Do you have any ideas on areas for improvement at the park?* There's a big difference between being able to complain about something and actually devising a solution. You want a solutions-oriented person. We have great luck with pastors, retired pastors, and retired military. Those guys rock. They know how to deal with people, they know how to lead, and they know how to take action.

4. *What do you think of the other tenants?* Obviously, the answer tells you more about the candidate than the other tenants. If they hate everybody, it's not going to work out.

5. *Our manager's application includes a request for a criminal and background check, as well as references. Will you have any challenges providing this information?*

As an added tip, visit the potential manager's home to find out what his or her home or car looks like. If the home is an absolute wreck, your park will likely be trashed too. I met with an onsite manager once, and his place was a disaster. I could barely navigate from the front door to the kitchen table. Then I walked the park and everybody had debris outside their homes, stacked right up to their steps. What you tolerate, you encourage. If the person's place is a dump, they are disqualified in my book.

Good Compensation Is Good Oversight

We have really good managers because we have a good process and great incentives. We provide the template. All they have to do to succeed is follow it. Whatever you do, don't pay managers a base salary of $1,000 or $1,200 a month with nothing contingent on performance. Your expenses are going to go through the roof, your occupancy will be terrible, and rent collection will be worse, because why would they care? They get paid no matter what. The formula for success is to streamline and simplify the job itself, pay fairly for the managers' time, then offer performance-based incentives. You want them to make money when you make money. This makes the achievement of your goals their goal.

We offer a base salary plus commission at several of our parks. On a park of sixty units, you might want to offer something like $150 as a base pay and then 5 percent of gross rents collected and deposited by a specific date. After that date, the percentage goes down. Recently at one of our parks, the management team put in an incredible amount of effort in order to get twenty-three units rehabbed

> You want them to make money when you make money. This makes the achievement of your goals their goal.

and up and running. Why did they work so hard? When those units were all rented, the manager earned 5 percent of all additional revenue. That's $1,000 per month extra *ongoing* for a little hard work. Like we do, they get the chance to increase their income by increasing performance. During the recession, how many low-wage workers got a $1000 per month raise?

I believe in hard work, and I believe in a business model that isn't dependent on a gangbuster economy. Just because the economy crashes doesn't mean your income needs to crash with it.

Offering incentives to earn money is fun, motivating, and confidence-building for managers. It also gets them thinking more like entrepreneurs. In most cases, they have been on the wrong side of the success equation their whole lives, where their compensation equaled less than their efforts. Our system offers a new perspective—more effort is rewarded with more pay. That's good math. I'd like to think that working on our team not only empowers them but also opens their eyes to a bigger picture of how economics can finally work in their favor. Treat everybody right, and everybody will be on your team.

Change Is Good

We like to turn stereotypes on their heads, especially the "absentee landlord" or "slumlord" stereotype. Investors often assume tenants will hate you if you come in and change things around. True, you may get a few grumblers. But it all depends on your intentions. When you think of yourself as a guardian of a community, I promise your results will be exponentially better than the park owner who goes in with the intention of getting blood from a turnip.

We see no difference between improving profits and improving the community. As soon as the new manager is in place, we send out a letter to tenants to present the transition as a positive thing so they recognize, "Wow, this community is going to be safer for my kids." We like to implement our neighborhood watch program and kick that off by hosting a community spring/fall cleaning day where we bring in a giant dumpster for removing large debris and have a contest for the best yard. This makes the tenants happy and helps the manager rent and sell more homes. They see that it is in everybody's interest to keep the place looking great. This, in turn, makes our managers' jobs much easier, which they always appreciate.

Management Handbook

I recommend you put together a management handbook that includes responsibilities on both the business side and the human side of the job.

On the business side

- Rental applications

- Leases

- Rent-to-own documents

- A copy of the park community rules

- A three-day notice to vacate

- The ten-day notice of nonpayment

- Demand letters

- Rule-violation notices

- Warning notices

- Forms for tenants who sign up for automated collections

- An indemnification form for subcontractors to sign when they work onsite. Make sure your manager knows to get a copy of the contractor's certificate of insurance when they fill out the indemnification.

- A copy of the fair housing handbook. Acknowledgement of receipt should be part of the management agreement. This way, if they violate any housing laws, knowingly or not, you won't be held liable for their actions.

Of course, we pull all these documents from our document library we have built over the years and, honestly, spent tens of thousands of dollars compiling. I recommend investing in a notebook computer so the manager has easy access to online tools you want them to work with. If you make the investment and teach them the few things they need to know on the computer, your life will be so much easier. Rather than be tied to an office phone and fax, you can run your company from your cell phone and laptop anywhere in the world.

So what do managers do to deserve the compensation package? Here are some other basic duties and responsibilities:

- Act as your salesperson, answering the phone, getting people out to see the property, showing the property, and signing rental leases.

- Enforce park rules, for the protection of both the tenants and the owners.

- Make it a place where tenants want to live, making sure that it's clean and safe.

- Monitor maintenance personnel, inspecting their work to ensure you are getting what you're paying for.

- Notify you when there are any utility issues and handle them as instructed by you.

- Clean vacant homes and prep them for renting/ selling.

On the human side:

- **Start on the right foot with new residents.** The manager makes new tenants feel welcome, answers any concerns, and ensures that every new tenant signs a copy of the lease, a copy of the park rules, and a copy of financial obligations. By going over the rules with new tenants, a manager makes his or her job a lot easier down the road.

- **Lead periodic park meetings or send out a newsletter with notices and updates.** Some managers/ owners only communicate with their tenants when it's time to raise the rent. There is not much pride of community in those parks. It's so much easier to make changes or get things done in the park when you stay connected to your tenants. Give the managers freedom to improve things. We like our managers to share park news and educational forums like disaster preparedness trainings and neighborhood watch updates. By the way, these really do help keep crime down and create cohesiveness within the community. Additionally, a lot of managers have really big hearts and they want to organize events and entertainments. One of our managers, recognizing that a lot of families in the park were barely scraping by, organized a holiday toy drive, which was a huge success. Those kids had a great Christmas, as it was for all of us who participated. We also do a yard competition in September and a party for Halloween, all to keep the tenants and manager engaged and "on the same side," so to speak.

- **Handle evictions.** If you let some folks pay their rent late, then others won't feel the same obligation to pay on time. A manager must serve notices or may even represent you in court. Tenants have to pay in order to stay. If they do not pay, they will receive an eviction notice. It's important to be very firm and consistent.

- **Increase and maintain occupancy rate.** We take care of advertising, while the manager needs to field calls and conduct home tours. Our incentive programs are designed to encourage initiative and creativity. We want them to have a sense of ownership. In a decent market, your manager can add two to four tenants per month. If you wonder how long it will take to get your income growing, use that number as a guide—add those additional rents. If you're buying a park with twenty vacancies, you cannot expect to fill the park in two months, but you might within the first half of the year. There are many variables here.

- **Initiate home sales.** Perhaps most important in terms of increasing profits is to initiate a conversation about home sales with every renter, every month. We train them to keep the sales pitch very simple and basic: "Hey, you know you're paying your rent on time. Those same payments could go toward your home." It's one of our biggest goals to turn more renters into homeowners, to get them invested in their future and their equity. I will explain this in greater depth in the next chapter about profit-generating strategies. As you have probably already guessed, it's another win-win scenario.

Managing the Managers

We know an investor who purchased a park and was clearly naïve. She hired a handyman, who charged her $10,000 per home to do his work, and she didn't set up adequate systems or visit the park for over six months after it was first purchased. Seeing that the landlord was inattentive, the manager bought materials at Lowe's, sent receipt copies to her, got reimbursed, then took those items right on back to Lowe's for a cash refund. Over the six-month period, the owner spent about $100,000. I estimate that about $40,000 actually went to the property.

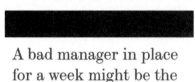

A bad manager in place for a week might be the cost of doing business. A bad manager in place for six months could cost you the business and is an indicator that you are an equally bad manager.

That is an expensive way to learn that you need to manage the manager. A bad manager in place for a week might be the cost of doing business. A bad manager in place for six months could cost you the business and is an indicator that you are an equally bad manager.

Greater Oversight Is Greater Profits

As Ronald Regan said, "Trust, but verify." Having management systems are imperative, but having redundant systems are key. We have built secondary systems that alert us if our primary systems are not being followed. It doesn't matter if you have the best system in the world if no one is following it. You need to take preventive measures. Here are some helpful tools that keep managers accountable:

- **Phone.** If you use Vonage for your phone service, you can see your call history from anywhere. It shows the duration of a call, where it's coming from, and more. A quick look at the online record shows if your manager is a Chatty Cathy on your billable hours. Vonage is also nice because you can establish a local phone number, as 800-numbers are too corporate and impersonal looking for this business.

- **Oversight checklist.** There is a direct correlation between a manager's activity and the park's results, so we have a daily checklist that helps us manage both activities and results. Our park managers are called every morning to ask for details on phone calls, home sales, and any other pressing issues they need to keep us apprised of. We go over the entire list. At the end of the day, our team calls and we go through everything that was assigned earlier in the day. That's how the work gets done, call by call, month by month. Mobile home parks that are run correctly can generate a significant amount of net income per month. Thirty minutes a day spent on the phone managing the property is time well spent.

- **Surprise visits.** We let managers know upfront we will drop in periodically. In the beginning, we'll drop in about every six weeks. Once things are humming along, we drop back to about quarterly. Of course, as our business has grown, we've added people who visit properties for us. A few years back, we bought a park from a couple who were looking to retire. Once they retired, they realized their retirement wasn't all it was cracked up to be. We stayed in touch with them, as we do with many of our sellers, and ended up hiring them to serve as regional managers over three of our parks. They are part of the team that assists us in onsite visits to keep the property managers on their toes.

When you've got all of these oversight tools working, your business risk drops dramatically. They don't guarantee that somebody won't try to take advantage of you, but you'll catch it and you'll catch it in due time. They also keep the manager focused on activities that matter most.

The best way to avoid firing a manager is to hire well, train well, and monitor their work. However, it does happen sometimes that you hire someone who isn't right for the job. We set clear expectations from the start and communicate whenever we don't feel a manager is living up to those expectations. When they're not doing a good job, they know it, and they leave somewhat amicably.

When you have to fire someone for stealing or lying, that's a different situation. Change the locks on the office, any storage buildings, and whatever park-owned homes the former manager may have had access to. Notify all vendors and other relevant parties, like the local lumber company or your appliance dealer. And make sure the phone and utility companies know this person has no authority over the property any longer.

As you form long-term, trustworthy relationships with your onsite managers and eventually hire a midlevel manager, depending on your scale, oversight becomes a well-oiled machine. It is liberating to know all systems are up and running. You can focus on maximizing profits. Wealth is not everything we want from life, but it's certainly what we expect from our business. In the next chapter, I'll explain some of the things we do to build the profitability of our mobile home park business.

Chapter 11

Give and Gain Advantage

Sarah's pen hovered over the piece of paper. Before signing her name, she looked up to smile at her husband, Richard. They had worked many years for this moment. He worked at a local graveyard, keeping the grounds and overseeing the burials. Her job was around-the-clock, too. For the last eight years, she had raised her two daughters full-time. This was a priceless moment she wanted to remember. They shared with us they never thought they would be able to own their own home.

When they first visited one of our mobile home parks and our manager told them about our lease-to-own program to assist renters in becoming homeowners, Sarah and Richard were excited about this opportunity from the beginning. They understood the benefits of owning their own home and immediately followed up with the onsite manager to find out more about the lease-to-own program. Our manager discussed with them how the program worked and emphasized that the payments they would be making to own their home would be comparable to the monthly rent they were currently paying.

Richard made a decent living, but they never seemed to be able to save or get ahead. Now they had something to work toward. The goal gave them hope for a better future for their girls. A few months later, when they got a sizable tax return, they decided it was time. Instead of watching that lump sum disappear on nothing special, they came to see our manager about using their tax return as their option money to start the lease-option process for their home. The day of ownership had finally arrived. Now their two little girls, eight and six, were running around and around the dining room table, singing, "Mommy and Daddy are buying us our own home!"

Ryan and I are not onsite at the parks every time a home is sold in our parks, but we happened to be onsite that day. And it was incredibly rewarding to be able to watch firsthand this couple taking hold of their part of the American Dream: home ownership. Their daughters were only six and eight, but they understood the pride of home ownership in their own way. It meant stability, no more moving around, and staying at the same school with the same friends.

We took photos of the couple together with their girls and the purchase agreement in front of their new home. They were so proud. This was one of those moments when Ryan and I knew for sure we were in the right business. Not only were we building a profitable business, but we were able to serve the people in the mobile home park communities that we owned by helping them take the next step toward a better life financially.

> Selling the homes generates income, increases the value of the property, and reduces expenses.

We could talk for days about how good it feels to help other people, but if helping other people hurts you, it is not a net positive—not a win-win. We are looking to achieve win-win opportunities in all of our business transactions. So if you are reading this thinking, *Well, that sounds wonderful, but wouldn't selling the mobile homes to the tenants reduce my long-term income on the property and make it less valuable?* the answer to that question is no. We have already discussed that lenders do not value the homes or the personal property; they value the property by the income derived from the lots. By selling the homes, we are removing ourselves from mobile home ownership (personal property), as well as all of the expenses that go with it. By creating a community of homeowners, the park will immediately experience the benefits of a pride of ownership in the community. A park that is better taken care of is more attractive to prospective tenants. This improves the value by increasing the occupancy.

Yes, this may lower our gross income that we were receiving from combining lot rent plus home rent, but it also significantly reduces our costs. This in turn increases the overall net income the park produces. Selling the homes generates income, increases the value of the property, and reduces expenses, while assisting your residents in experiencing home-ownership.

Wealth is not a result of taking advantage but giving it.

Help the Working Poor Become Homeowners

We love this aspect of investing because we love the opportunity to serve our clientele while making the transaction profitable for us as well. The thrill of watching someone buy their own home is equally as exciting as teaching individuals about the benefits of investing. We get to watch them thrive and achieve a level of financial success for the first time in their lives.

This approach of converting the tenants to homeowners is truly a business advantage. Our parks have more stability while unloading a lot of overhead expenses when the tenants own their own homes. If the park is responsible for rented homes, then we never hear the end of air-conditioning problems, soft floors, leaky faucets, etc. And renters do not take care of the property in the way that homeowners do.

This brings up another major issue—turnover. Someone who is renting a mobile home may stay for years, but more likely than not it is a few months. And oftentimes a person who is there for only a few months will leave behind the damage and repair costs that an owner will have to absorb before they are able to make it produce income again. This is one of the most unique concepts of mobile home ownership. If done correctly, it is essentially renting dirt. Dirt cannot call you about a broken air conditioner. Dirt cannot call you about the doorknob or the faucet. The dirt draws income called lot rent.

This is not to say that a mobile home park that doesn't have any park-owned homes or has sold them off has no expenses. It does. But the day-to-day maintenance requests concerning home repairs that run up your material and labor costs are significantly reduced when you help your tenants purchase their own homes.

If your park has no park-owned homes, you can focus on the general upkeep of the property, landscaping, roads, occupancy, management, and collections of lot rent. Of course, this is assuming the park owner is not involved with the utilities and that all utilities are provided completely by the city.

You may be wondering, *So, what is the ideal situation?*

- Lot rent parks
- No park-owned homes
- Sub-metered utilities managed by the city
- Paved roads
- Onsite management
- Good location with long-term growth prospects

You may not always be able to find this exact situation when you are buying. Or you may find all of these, except the owner of the park also owns some of the homes. This isn't a deal breaker, but it is a reality that you will have to deal with. If you purchase a mobile home park where the owner also owns some of the homes, your goal would be to sell those homes as quickly as possible. If the park is already fully occupied, this should be relatively easy, as you can sell the homes to the current tenants. The sale of these homes will eliminate a major headache on your end. It's also a huge opportunity to assist someone else in becoming a homeowner.

Think about it. By providing seller financing, we can turn tenants into homeowners without changing their monthly payments. Instead of paying, for example, $150 per month in lot rent and $350 per month for the rental home, they put $500–$2,000 down and pay $200 per month lot rent and $300 on their lease-to-own payment. You make an upfront lump sum of cash and increased the value of the park and future cash flow by raising pad rent. You also reduced your maintenance liabilities. The tenants, who might have needed years to save up for homes, get their foot in the door by being able to purchase the homes from the parks through payments. When they're ready to move on, the homeowners are responsible for selling their own homes. If you think there is no way they can come up with a down payment, watch them. You've just given them an opportunity no one else will give them. They find the money. You want the tenants to "put skin in the game" and have some commitment. You are looking for a down payment to show that commitment. The home may be worth $7,000 to $20,000. Odds are, they don't have good credit or a lot of extra cash or they most likely wouldn't be in your park. You have to bear that in mind when negotiating. That doesn't mean you should give the home away; it is your asset and has value. Just be realistic about where you are both coming from financially and your end goal—to have the tenants own their own homes and be responsible for the upkeep.

"Pride of ownership" is an overused term, but it still hasn't lost its power to motivate. Lending is hard enough on a house without wheels; imagine someone with bad credit and very little cash trying to walk in and get a loan on a home with wheels. If your tenants own their own homes, you will bring in less income than if you rented out the homes. However, you have significantly reduced your expenses and eliminated the headache of maintaining those homes. Our long-term goal is to be in a 100 percent land-lease position, collecting lot rents only.

The Handyman Special

Selling rental homes to tenants improves occupancy long-term, thus reducing your expenditures on advertising and costs associated with turning a home. Sometimes it even makes sense to practically give the homes away. Give houses away for free? Okay, go ahead and charge them a dollar. Let me explain.

The previous owner's deferred maintenance might help you buy a park for less, but you still have to deal with the declining condition of the existing homes. Many mobile homes can be rehabbed for relatively little money, from $500 to $2000 each. If you do the rehab yourself in order to get a renter moved in, you are fronting the cash required for materials and labor as well as spending your most valuable asset—time. If a prospective renter comes in and is interested in living there, you can offer them "the handyman special." This is where we sell a home as-is for as little as one dollar to the types of tenants who want to own long-term and who are able to do the rehab work personally or are willing to pay for it themselves. All of a sudden, you've got lot rent coming in on something that would otherwise have been a time-consuming expense.

This is not something we do frequently, but it is a strategy we use if we have a few homes in bad shape and we don't want to invest the time and capital to get them ready to sell. So, it's not a primary strategy, as you run the risk of them starting a project and taking twelve months to complete it while you have agreed to free lot rent while they finish repairs. If you decide to offer the handyman special, you will need to be clear on the terms of how much time you will give them to complete repairs and when their first lot rent payment is due.

After all, you're not trying to reinvent these parks as luxury retreats. You just want to make each mobile home safe, clean, and functional. If you have multiple deals going on at the same time or you buy a park with quite a few fixer-upper homes, you might not want to sink the cash into all that maintenance at one time. Even a flyer at the local laundromat can turn your situation around. A house for a dollar? Who wouldn't jump at that? Plenty of renters are perfectly capable

The key word is owner-ship. People want to take care of what's theirs.

of replacing some rotten flooring, painting, or repairing the toilet. The only reason they *don't* usually do it is because they have no incentive. Suddenly, it's not *the* toilet, it's *their* toilet. Or it's their walls, their roof, their flooring. The key word is *ownership*. People want to take care of what's theirs. After the homes are sold, the land rents and home loan payments keep rolling in. This puts you in an excellent cash position that will only get better over time.

Plugging Profit Leaks

For a real-estate entrepreneur, mobile home parks are like a perfect storm of profit opportunity. They offer many opportunities for expense reduction as well as increased income. There are some relatively inexpensive ways to reduce costs, plug profit leaks, and create growth that I can share with you here.

Once Ryan and I had a few parks under our belts, we realized there were lots of little leaks in the larger picture of owning and managing a park over time. If we kept adding parks without plugging those leaks, it would add up to a significant amount of money lost. You can lose a little change out of your pocket one day and never notice it's missing. But if you lose that same small amount every day over the course of a year, it can be devastating. You can lose a substantial amount of money in this business by losing sight of small opportunities. It was time for us to streamline our business with effective systems.

Remote security cameras

As we began purchasing properties all across the country, the need for automated systems became increasingly important. Being the techie that he is, my husband devised a video surveillance system that he installed in a park we own in Kentucky. Once the cameras were installed throughout the park, in the office, and in the storage shed, we were amazed at how much it helped us in holding our manager's feet to the fire on a daily basis.

Of course, we don't sit around and watch our managers and tenants every minute of the day, but the point is that we are able to if we would like to. At any given moment, either one of us can look at our phone and see our properties from a variety of angles, whether we're on the road for business or home by the lake. It's peace of mind in the palm of your hand. The mobile home park owner should not be concerned if the cameras bother the manager. Business is business. Remember, if you run your business like a business, you will make business money. If you run it like a hobby, it will most likely cost you money.

How do security cameras increase our profits? Think about this:

- We know the manager is in the office and not missing the opportunity to answer the phone or show the property.

- We know how the manager is performing on the job and can identify problems early.

- We know how the tenants are treating the property.

- We know maintenance is being kept current.

- We know when tenants are coming by the office.

- It eliminates the concern about the office time, the condition of the property, and prospective tenants visiting the property.

Good managers

Strong onsite and offsite property management is going to be the key to your success as a mobile home park owner. In this area of your business, it is crucial that you utilize a consistent system. In the previous chapter, we discussed a manager's checklist and a management manual, and both of these tools keep the owner and the onsite manager on track with specific goals and tasks for each day.

For example, the log of incoming calls we access from our phone service provider shows us whether our park managers are getting calls on the property or not—if not, we need to improve our advertising strategy. If the manager is getting plenty of calls but not showing units, we may need to work on the manager's phone personality or give them a script which prioritizes making appointments or make sure they are accessible enough to show at times that are convenient for the prospective renters. If the managers do give home site tours to those callers but fail to rent or sell the units, we need to work on their sales ability or the property's condition.

As the owner watching out for the bottom line, your job is to make sure your manager consistently answers the phone, returns calls, shows units, and keeps the property clean and safe. You can manage the advertising from afar, but in order to do this effectively, you must be managing your manager correctly. An engaged manager makes all the difference between rising profits and stag-nation or profit losses.

Legal documents

As a friend of ours always says, "When you buy the best, you only cry once." So start out with the right contracts and documents from the beginning. An extremely valuable aspect of our business that allows us to be systematic in our approach is our ever-growing document library. We have a document library that consists of all the documents that we need to run our business successfully. We have spent a significant amount of money in attorney's fees having our documents drafted correctly, but I am confident that it has saved us multiples of that number.

The value in these documents is not just that they have been drafted with great detail and attention. They also provide for consistency in our investments. Each property has the documents and resources that it needs to operate correctly on a daily, monthly, and annual basis. We maintain purchase-and-sale agreements, addendums, seller-financing documents, assignment of contracts, leases, notices, and much more. Good operating documents are well worth the upfront investment because they prevent all kinds of profit leaks related to evictions, rent increases, and other potential contractual hassles.

Good operating documents are well worth the upfront investment because they prevent all kinds of profit leaks.

You will pay more to get the best business tools and contracts, but they are worth every penny. Don't order generic contracts online just because they're cheap. I am talking about lease agree-ments, mortgage agreements, purchase-and-sale agreements, and other related documents that you will want to run the business profitably. They may save you on your upfront costs, but all of the headaches, hassles, and cost of dealing with ineffective documents after the fact will most likely cost you more than if you would have just done the things right the first time.

Reducing costs

As you recognize by now, there is a significant amount of opportunity in the MHP investment space. Much of the opportunity is in improving the income side of the business while reducing operational expenses. These areas of opportunity should be readily apparent to you during the due-diligence phase of acquisitions.

Utilities

When I first started investing in mobile home parks and learning all the ins and outs unique to this investment, a seller convinced me I would lose a lot of tenants if I made them pay for their own water and sewer expense. I didn't want to take a big occupancy hit right up front, so I followed his suggestion on this. I knew he had owned the park for more than twenty years, and he probably knew more about this than I did.

However, I quickly learned this was not wise advice. He had looked at the circumstances from his perspective. He lived a few minutes from the property and ran it himself. He did not mind talking to tenants individually about their utility usage and charging tenants various amounts if they were using more. There was no process to this approach, and we could not duplicate it. The decision was made to sub-meter the utilities and bill it back directly to the tenants. It became the responsibility of the tenants to pay for

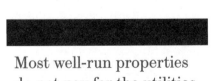

Most well-run properties do not pay for the utilities. It is the responsibility of the tenants.

their utilities. It was our intention to continue to grow our business and create as much duplication in the process as possible. One of these processes required tenants to pay for their own utilities.

With more experience, I realized the seller was wrong—people don't move. They know if they live anywhere else they will have to pay their own utilities. Experience also showed us utility usage is reduced by up to 25–30 percent when tenants are personally responsible for their own bills. Showers get shorter, and the hoses aren't left running in the street during a car wash smoke break. It makes sense. Ownership brings with it a sense of responsibility.

Just how much does it improve income? Let's look at an example of an MHP we purchased with one master water meter and the following details:

- Fifty lots at $250 per month in lot rent = $12,500 in monthly income.
- The water/sewer bill was $1,900 per month.

We decided to sub-meter the property and have all tenants billed directly. As the owner, we have the upfront cost of sub-metering. However, this decision increases our net income by approximately $22,800 a year, as well as increasing the value of the property for resale. At a 10 percent capitalization rate, the increase of value to the park is $228,000.

Occupancy rates

The sweet spot when buying is a cash-flow-positive park with some room to grow. If you buy a park that is 100 percent tenant-owned and occupied, you may have paid a premium price and have no room to grow. (This is certainly okay, as there is lot of value in stability.) A fully-occupied park will not put the same demand on your time as one that has some room to grow. If your research showed that every other park in the area is 95 percent occupied and the one you're looking at is 70 percent occupied, get it under contract. The demand in the market certainly seems to be there, and if it passes due diligence, you will be able to benefit from the market by increasing occupancy and therefore increasing your income and value or equity. Of course, you want to create more profit potential. You will also want to ask these questions:

- Why is the occupancy so low? Is it management? Location? Something else?

- Are there vacant or abandoned homes? How many?

- Are there vacant lots? How many?

- Why are the homes vacant? Do they need work or has the current owner neglected to advertise? If the homes need work, a basic work order with a timeline and budget is required before getting started.

- What is the current lot rent?

- What is the current home rent?

Is buying a park that has growth potential going to fill itself? No. However, these first few steps will get your park going in the right direction. Hire and train a manager to show the park, sell the homes, improve the basic appearance of the park, and run advertising with incentives.

Rent increases

If the current park owner has not raised rents in a long time, which we see is often the case, it's a good idea to initiate the rent increase upon closing. Investors are always afraid that increasing the rents will cause people to move out. The reality is that we charge fair-market rent. If it isn't currently fair market, then it's unfair market, and that is unfair for you. When I am asked if tenants will leave you when you raise the rents, I always smile. If I am charging fair-market rent, they will only move to pay the same somewhere else. If you don't like the idea of making the rent increase as the new owner, you can build a rent increase into your purchase-and-sale agreement. It could say something like, "Closing to take place thirty days after seller raises rents to $_____ per lot." That way, the seller notifies tenants and executes the change before you ever even enter the picture. Any tenant resentment over the increase is aimed at him, not you. After that, we maintain rent rates with current fair-market value.

Rent increases will contribute significantly to your bottom line. It is important to mention that if you purchase an income-producing property and fail to increase your rents each year, you will one day lose money when you factor in inflation.

Rent increases are one of those great income opportunities. How much does it cost to increase rents? Nothing. Someone might mention, "Well, you lose a few people." The reality is, you may. But let's assume you have a fifty-unit park at $250 lot rent and the fair-market value is $275. Let's also assume 92 percent occupancy (that's forty-six units occupied). That's means your park is currently grossing $11,500 when you should be grossing $12,650. That additional $1,150 a month is $13,800 a year increase in income. If you happen to lose a tenant or two, you will still be ahead of the game. The other reality is that you are moving them to fair-market value, not above fair market. So why would a tenant move if they're going to pay the same amount somewhere else? It costs money to move.

You may have a few threats or rumors of people moving if rents are increased, but if you look at the cost to move a mobile home, you'll understand it costs an average of $2,000 to move the home out of your park to another one. Most tenants don't want to incur that added expense and move out, only to pay the same amount of rent somewhere else.

Section 8 housing

Section 8, a subsidized-housing program provided by the United States Department of Housing and Urban Development, provides tenants who qualify with a subsidy that will assist them in making their monthly rental payments. These amounts, approved by the government, are to be used toward a tenant's rent and sent directly to the landlord on the tenant's behalf. Being in the business of mobile home parks, we are naturally working in affordable housing. We provide affordable housing for low-income families who self-pay, as well as some who receive government assistance. For our tenants who receive government assistance, we receive the rental portion from the government wired into our bank account on the first business day of each month.

Think about the advantages of this. HUD actually promotes your parks by listing vacancies for their aid recipients, the rent payment is guaranteed and automated, and the tenant is motivated to follow the park rules to maintain their eligibility.

It's true that HUD tenants are renters and not homeowners. You wouldn't sell the home to the tenant in this scenario, which should be your long-term goal for maximized profit and minimized migraines. However, we've found that HUD tenants create a solid income stream that is wired to our accounts monthly. These tenants are typically long-term in our experience and care for their homes the way a homeowner would, due to the regular inspections conducted by the HUD office. Because these tenants are monitored carefully, due to their financial assistance, you will most likely not experience some of the issues that occur with a self-pay renter. It is also important to note that there is a portion of the rental amount that the tenant is responsible for. That specific dollar amount is determined by HUD and communicated to you and the tenant.

Assignment fee

Over the years, when we meet investors seeking certain types of deals, we would take their names down so that in case our researchers happened to find those types of deals, we could pass along the deals to them. Meanwhile, in our travels we often find great opportunities that don't quite fit into what we are looking for but are good deals all the same. We finally mixed the chocolate in the peanut butter and got a really sweet deal. We connected the buyers with the sellers whose properties fit their criteria, and we assign the contracts for a fee equal to the net monthly income times ten. We've done contract assignments anywhere from $5,000 to $30,000 and even up to $80,000!

Remember, as we discussed earlier in the book, all you have to do to make a contract assignable—even if it says it is not assignable—is to handwrite your name plus "and/or assigns" on the buyer's line of a contract or purchase-and-sale agreement. For example, the buyer's line of the agreement should read, "Scott Johnson and/or assigns..."

Whether or not we expect to assign the contract, we need the ability to assign the buyer to a different entity. We do not close on mobile home parks in our personal names. Each property is held separately in its own company name. When we put a property under contract, we have not yet opened the company for this acquisition because we have not decided that we are going to close on it at the time we put it under contract. Because we do not create the limited liability corporation (LLC) that will own the property until the end of the due-diligence period, we don't actually know the name of the buyer at the time we execute the contract.

Summary of Financing Options

When we discussed creative financing earlier, the main point was that options like seller financing make the deal *possible*. It also happens that creative financing can make the deal cheaper, due to reduced closing costs and unnecessary fees. In addition to setting favorable interest rates, we can contract for delayed first payments and various balloon dates that are suitable to us on the loan.

The four basic scenarios for financing are:

1. Seller financing

2. Some combination of seller and conventional financing

3. Conventional financing

4. A much less common option that includes the use of a private placement offering (PPO) to raise cash for the down payment

Whichever one you choose depends on the specifics of each deal and the willingness of the seller to participate. Our first, best offer is usually based on seller financing because that produces the best results for both the buyer and the seller. Our lowest offer is cash, because that's the one that costs us the most. But we don't make offers based on financing options per se. We make offers based on the return we want to generate. Of course, various financing options and down payment requirements impact that return.

In a nutshell, a PPO is a kind of investment fund. You invite qualified investors to put cash into a venture in exchange for an annual return and a portion of ownership. There's far more to it than this, and I don't have the space to deal with it here except to mention it to you for your own personal research. For any further information, you can go to www.sec.gov.

I hope you have seen throughout this book that you can unlock the hidden profits in mobile home parks with a whole ring of different keys. To start, you find the opportunities that you know how to turn into great deals. Then you reduce your expenses and increase gross revenues to fulfill the property's potential. The approach I've described in this book, from identifying markets and parks through cash-flow analysis, contracts, financing, due diligence, management, and profit generation, serves as a model for building a herd of cash cows.

Let Our Experience Help You

You may be wondering why we're giving away all of our secrets. We don't feel threatened by someone's desire to be involved in this business. There is no mobile home park fairy out there. We've been a part of enough deals to know there is not a shortage of opportunity in the marketplace. If you're interested in investing, we want to help you do it the right way. It's a lot less expensive and a lot less time consuming if you can peek over the shoulder of someone who has already done what you want to do.

> I think the real estate market as a whole is viewed negatively, which has provided an incredible opportunity for those of us who want to invest rather than speculate.

Ryan and I have done a significant amount of learning on the job due to the lack of available resources out there in our areas of business. We have also met plenty of people who try to pretend they know what they are talking about, when they have very little genuine experience. We have seen these mouthpieces wreak financial havoc on many newbies. If this book can help those who are willing to work have a more efficient path toward financial success, then it has achieved its purpose.

One of our goals is to help people get where they want to go in the fastest and most efficient way. It's our hope that when you achieve your goals, you will take the time to help someone else so this process of wealth development will be a blessing to you, your sphere of influence, and our country overall. Yes, that is a long-range goal, but it's one that is important to us in our business.

Chances are, you've not met my husband or me, so I want to explain how we feel about sharing our investment methods with you:

1. The knowledge and experience we have acquired is viewed as an absolute blessing.

2. We feel honored and rewarded to be able to serve and enable others to prosper right along with us.

3. We believe that to whom much is given, much is required. We will continue to give and share as the opportunity is available to us, and we hope our behavior will be met with a domino effect.

I think the real-estate market as a whole is viewed negatively, which has provided an incredible opportunity for those of us who want to invest rather than speculate. Frankly, with more than fifty thousand mobile home parks across the United States, we're not concerned about the money drying up!

True leadership will help other people succeed in their goals. That said, Ryan and I derive a great deal of personal fulfillment by creating strategies for increasing *other people's* profits—and that means you! I hope that as you close this book you feel you've been both inspired and educated to begin to invest in MHPs. You can expect hard work with a lot of joy and satisfaction thrown in. Most of all, it's my sincere hope that your cash flow will produce significant income for your family and that one day you'll pass this book to a friend and help them to succeed in their financial goals too.

Chapter 12

Building Your Business and Leaving a Legacy

Now what?
Now that you've read this book, what can you do in your own life to increase your business objectives and pour into the lives of others?

Ryan and I wanted to share our experience because we believe in giving back. Mentoring others and helping people achieve their dreams is at the core of everything we do, and it's our hope that once you begin to apply the principles we've shared from our own journey of investing and owning mobile home parks that your business will begin to multiply. It will be hard work, but the rewards will be greater than anything you could possibly imagine.

When we speak at seminars or teach the principles of business ownership to others, we don't gloss over the reality that in order to be successful, you should plan to work hard. We believe that when you begin with that mindset, you're prepared to do the heavy lifting and will be more committed to your business success and less willing to give up. There's no magic pill for success, and the inspirational gurus who teach that there is are only doing a disservice to everyone!

Building a business that gives back is like an athlete training to compete in a race.

When you think about building your own mobile home park business, remember that it's not enough just to enter the race. The goal is to finish strong! And to finish the race strong, you've got to have the right attitude, inspiration, and tools. Just like a world-class Olympic athlete who prepares for competition, you've got to be prepared to train, endure, build strength, and take the necessary steps to win—because your business is your life, and the time you spend in it affects your personal life, too. Investing in your business is a daily process, and it should be joyful and satisfying, not stressful and grinding.

What Does Building a Successful Legacy Mean to You?

As I said before, one of our goals in business is to help people get where they want to go in the fastest and most efficient way. That's a big part of our legacy. Efficiency is important in every aspect of your life because when you're working smarter, you have clarity about what you want and the steps you need to take every day to get there. Why take longer to do something than you need to? That only wastes valuable time and money. It diminishes return.

Take time to think about what you really want out of your business and life. When you build your business, build it around the core values you believe in because when you keep your beliefs and values at the heart of your daily activities, everything flows out from that. Your legacy develops naturally from your belief system. Your legacy is built from the habits you live out daily, the way you mentor others, the business you build, and the individuals and generations you impact. As you build your MHP business, take time to consider what your core values are. You might even decide to write out a mission statement or keep a list of the top five things that matter to you posted above your desk or on a wall, visible to everyone in your business.

For Ryan and I, our core values (the things that are at the heart of our business and legacy) center on ethics, people, relationships, and integrity.

Business Ethics

Every business has a culture, and it's pretty easy to tell how the owners think and believe by the way their employees act. Chances are, you've encountered a cranky, rude, or downright arrogant employee at the airline counter, restaurant, or hotel check-in desk while traveling, and it certainly leaves a lasting impression. When that happens to us, I tend to wonder about the business owner and the type of culture they've created. In a business where several employees are rude, you wonder if they're getting any training at all on customer service, or if the business even cares about the customer.

If there were a motto that summed up our personal philosophy on business ethics, it would be "Do unto others as you would have them do unto you." It's commonly known as the Golden Rule, and it's something we have all heard before. But it takes intention-ality to live by it—especially when a tenant or someone else you interact with is being increasingly difficult! Sometimes the easiest way to respond isn't always the best. It's easy to say something sharp, hurtful, or defensive, but that's not the way you'd want others to treat you, and it doesn't foster strong relationships or positive business impressions.

When I was growing up, my mom repeatedly told me that I should treat others the way I wanted to be treated. She didn't present this as an option—this is the way it was in her house, and it's a rule that has been ingrained into my DNA. But the Golden Rule wasn't the only thing she taught me. She also told me that if I was a good steward of what I had been given, I would be blessed with more. This is the blessing in the application of the Golden

Rule. The benefits of operating your business in a win-win type approach will always have a positive impact on the business.

I always find it funny how many people think that people who use the Golden Rule are weak. I can't tell you how many businesses I've seen that have ignored this rule, and while they may have had a meteoric rise, many of them had a colossal collapse. I would rather grow a business slowly, guided by values that respect the dignity of every life, than to grow quickly on the backs of those we should be serving. Many have made more money than we have, but it's been important for us to build it, keep it, and invest in the lives of others along the way. There's no magic pill. It's a lifelong process. When you give back, you'll find that your giving is force multiplied by strengthening your personal and business relationships.

The Power of Relationships

People tend to think about the word *relationships* in a personal sense, but in reality, if you're engaging in business with someone regularly, you're building a relationship. It might be a short-term business relationship with a maintenance company or a long-term relationship with a tenant, but all interactions between the people you encounter matter. That tenant might recommend five more. That repairman you talked to for just a few minutes might work for someone else who could be influential to your life or business. Don't discount the value of people. Listen to them, and be intentional about the impression you're leaving behind. Remember that city worker I talked to when I was first getting started in the business? That led to other connections and an investment in a mobile home park I never would have known was available!

Ryan and I believe that the Golden Rule should be utilized both personally and professionally. A business is built on its people, and there's no designated place where the person ends and the business begins. It's a fluid transaction. So whether you plan to build a small business, a midsized one, or a major company, it's the human equity that matters. People are the lifeblood of any organization, and every success happens through them.

Your people create your business personality (otherwise known as its culture). Every single business, large or small, has a culture. Your culture (the way you think, act, and believe) is evident to everyone you interact with. Your employees will reflect your culture. What type of business culture will you build, and what values are at the heart of it?

I like to think that we're in the business of relationships. We help people, and they help us. At this point in my life, I realize that the value in everything is in a relationship. Despite being raised in the church, I am not religious. I am, however, relational, and I know that faith is a relationship with your Creator. Marriage is a relationship with your spouse. A business is a relationship with your clients, colleagues, and anyone you interact with in your daily business transactions. Relationships develop from one-on-one communication via telephone and e-mail. They develop face to face. Show me someone who is great at building relationships, and I'd be willing to bet that same person has a thriving network of business contacts. Be relational. If you don't think of yourself that way, work to develop the skills you need.

We value positive cash flow and the freedom that brings, but the heartbeat of the people in our company and the relationships we build reflect the Golden Rule in everything our organization thinks, does, and says. We believe that's vitally important for anyone building a business. Having said that, any business owner will feel a tremendous amount of pressure by that reality. If you do, that's a good thing! It means you have a

"Do unto others as you would have them do unto you." The Golden Rule should be utilized both personally and professionally.

conscience and also a desire to operate by the Golden Rule. If you don't feel a tug at that reality, you won't be in business for long.

Integrity and Leadership

You may be a business owner with a total staff of you, but you are still the leader of the way your business runs. You're in command of the way that ethics, business values, and customer interactions are managed. It doesn't matter how many people are on payroll; the concept of treating others the way you would like to be treated is not volume-based. It should be present in every person and transaction that takes place.

Let's not forget the foundational importance of honesty, fairness, respect, integrity, and loyalty. Telling the truth never gets old. Treating people fairly never goes out of style. We have seen repeatedly the blessings of operating a business by the "principle of reciprocity" firsthand in our own lives and businesses, as well as the lives and businesses of those that we interact with. And we've determined that we will not compromise on these values.

What are the things you aren't willing to compromise on? Whether we like it or not, as business owners we're automatically in a position of leadership. Are you congruent with the things you say and do at home and in your business life? Business ethics are top down in any organization, and the tone is set by the leadership. Guess what? That's you!

Monitor the Way You Think and Believe

As a business owner, your biggest asset is you. That's why it's important to monitor what comes into your life (and mind) and what goes out. What comes in is in reference to your thoughts, beliefs, and what you study, read, and learn. Are you a lifelong learner and earner? You can be! I know real-estate investors who didn't get started until very late in life.

What goes out and your ability to teach others is a reflection of everything inside of you. Business ownership is holistic, and everything the leader does affects the individual employees, tenants, partners, friends, family, and culture of that business. Monitor the way you think, and learn to recognize if there are any limiting beliefs or thought patterns that are holding you back. Some people wake up each day and think of all the things that could possibly go wrong. But when you start your day that way, you're setting yourself up for failure. Think positively, and don't dwell on worry or fear.

One of the most common barriers to success for any business owner is fear. Fear can literally cripple a business. The what-ifs can creep into your daily thought life and become a pattern that needs to be broken. *What if this happens, what if that happens*? Have you ever met someone who continually worried about the what-ifs? If you find yourself thinking about things that have not yet happened, *stop*. Break the chain of the what-if thinking and replace worry with an inspiring thought! Your business and your legacy begin with the way you think and believe. If you're holding onto worry or waking up thinking about problems or what-ifs, you're not thinking positive, inspiring thoughts that will help you prosper.

The what-ifs are a close cousin to the "I Don't Haves…" that we talked about in chapter 1. The "I Don't Have's…" tend to make excuses that prevent their success by focusing on the things they don't have before they even get started! A what-if mentality can be just as limiting because even people who have achieved a large measure of success as business owners can find themselves slipping into what-if thinking, instead of "anything is possible" thinking!

It's important to note here that we aren't suggesting the path to successful business ownership and growth is by wearing rose-colored glasses. Yes, it's important to be strategic and consider the roadblocks your business might face down the line. But what we are really emphasizing here is that you pay attention to your daily thoughts, just as you pay attention to your daily activities or bank account. The way you think creates power and fuel for your day, your business, and your life. Positive thoughts stem from a belief system that generates positive activity and a prosperous life.

What changes can you make today to increase your personal and financial legacy? A lot of books give you tactical steps about all the things you have to do to be successful. The seven steps to building wealth, the ten steps to losing weight, the five habits of highly effective humans—you get my drift. Yes, it's important to know what to do to increase your chances of reaching your goals, but I've been in business long enough to learn that it's also about the things you don't do.

> The way you think creates power and fuel for your day, your business, and your life.

Successful business owners don't make rash decisions, for instance. They think and plan and get clarity on the numbers before they decide to invest. Successful people don't take on a lot of non-value-added obligations, meetings, or time-sucking activities. While others might be out at networking events every week, the most successful business owners I've encountered tend to be more cautious and discerning about their time. When you're building your business and a legacy that will affect your bank account and your family, it's imperative to think about what you do as well as what you don't do.

Some of the most successful people you'll ever meet are also the most efficient because they've learned how to eliminate time-wasting activities and toxins from their lives. Is there someone, something, or some monthly obligation that's not adding but subtracting from your life? You don't have to work hard to know what that thing is. It's the habit, individual, or belief that creates stress in your life. Take time to think about how much more positive your business would be if you eliminated that stressor or invested your time elsewhere. If you're holding onto a truly toxic belief or investing energy in something destructive or negative, it's time to make a change.

It's Your Dream

I have to preface this next story by saying, look, it doesn't really matter what other people think. It doesn't matter if your Aunt Edna had a bad real-estate experience and lost her shirt on a rental property. It doesn't matter if your neighbor thinks real estate is the worst investment ever. It's your dream. And we are here to tell you that if you're willing to work hard, and smart, that you'll be able to invest in MHPs and get a positive return on your investment for a very long time. We've done it, and it's been a rewarding and profitable experience.

A lot of people throughout history have given up on their dreams because of their own fears or the negative opinions of naysayers. Don't be one of them.

Property Investment—Perception vs. Reality

I was on a property visit once, and on the flight down I sat next to a FedEx executive. He stated that he had to delay his retirement by roughly five years because of the economic downturn. If the economy takes another turn for the worse, he said he may be out of a job. He told me he had always wanted to invest in real estate but never got up the nerve to do it. That fascinated me, given the type of investment, acquisition, management, and sales decisions this man made every day at the company he worked for.

It is always interesting how many people can be so willing to build their employers' businesses but never consider doing it for themselves. Properly evaluating a property, running the numbers, structuring your contract, performing detailed due diligence, and having a management plan in place will reduce your risk in any transaction. But I am not in the risk-taking business. To me, working in corporate America can provide a perceivably comfortable and stable lifestyle, but the risk lies in the fact that your income is coming from one source you have very little control over. By learning to invest properly in cash-flow assets, I have learned how to reduce my risks so that my future isn't based on the whims or needs of any employer, or employers, in the future. Most people trade perceived security now for risk in the future, but the very same person will avoid action today because the risk is too great.

It's agonizing to think of all the families who have worked their whole lives, played by the rules, and saved for their retirement only to wake up one day and realize the rules to the game have changed. Suddenly the retirement money they were planning to live on, travel with, and leave as an inheritance to their families is not even enough for them to live on if they retire. It is a game-changer to realize you have to work another decade just to have enough to make it through retirement without being a burden to your family. This is one reason it's so important to build multiple streams of income. It's sad to sit down with couples as they go through this realization process. But the good news is that there is hope, and the key is to build out additional income streams.

Mobile home parks have the capability to deliver a very comfortable lifestyle to investors if they invest in them correctly. While many people have witnessed their 401k accounts take a nosedive, we've been blessed to see our business grow exponentially during that same period of time. So who is taking the greater risk—an executive at a company or an investor who has spread their risk over multiple investments? There's risk in everything, and you have to do what's right for you.

The Comfort Zone Isn't Very Comfortable

Don't be afraid of the opportunity ahead! Be prepared to put in some sweat equity, stay up from time to time to work late at night if you have to, and stretch beyond your comfort zone. I know plenty of people who spend their time on Facebook or surfing the internet for hours into the evening after the kids have gone to bed. You could be researching mobile home parks! The point is, we only have so many hours in the day to work with, but chances are you're capable of much more than you're doing right now.

At one of the very first mobile home parks we bought, I got to know one woman who, like my own mother, worked multiple jobs to provide the best for her kids. She had lived there for a long time, but previously she and her husband owned a house. He was working in construction when he was injured in a motorcycle accident. As is the case with so many Americans, that's when the hospital bills started piling up, and she started doing odd jobs. To save money and get out of debt, they moved into the park. We hired her as the park manager since she was well respected there and knew everything there was to know about the place. As manager, she got under people's mobile homes to help fix their plumbing and kept accurate accounting books all in the same day. She was an amazing woman! Not only was she adaptable enough to perform many tasks, but she took an obstacle and turned it into an opportunity.

As you move forward to develop your business, you'll be faced with obstacles along the way. But don't let that stop you. Continue working through them, and take steps each day to progress, move forward, and gain momentum. A lot of times the obstacles you'll encounter are from within! And the strategy for overcoming them is the same as with any other challenge. Move forward, keep the momentum going, and keep an "anything is possible" mindset.

Next Steps

By this point, you should be feeling energized, but it's also possible that you might be feeling a bit overwhelmed. You've got a lot of knowledge, and all sorts of aspirations and adrenaline, but you aren't quite sure how to take that next step. The best advice we can give you is to jump in. Take steps forward toward your business goals, and know that anything is possible. Take one step, then another, and keep the momentum going. Success is all about momentum. That means doing something each day to progress in the direction of your dream.

Is it your dream to own one MHP or perhaps a whole lot more? Is it your dream to own one to pass down to your children to manage for their own business? Maybe it is your dream to be the founder of a nonprofit organization that serves others in need. Maybe you don't care about mobile home parks at all, but your desire is to responsibly implement the strategy of investing in mobile home parks so that your profit can serve as the vehicle that will allow you to do what you love. It's your business, and you're in charge of how creative you want to get when it comes to giving back.

Although one barometer of your success will be increased cash flow, that's not the ultimate goal. The biggest success you can have is to have a positive impact by mentoring, building wealth, bringing freedom, and creating a ripple effect on your family, friends, and anyone else you mentor and teach. We get so much satisfaction when we witness a family buying their very first home and achieving the American Dream. It's a big benefit of the business we've worked hard to build because we can help others along the way, and the rewards of that are immediately evident. Selling the homes generates income, increases the value of the property, and reduces expenses, but it also assists residents in experiencing homeownership.

When you build your own business with that goal in mind, you're already on your way to prospering. What's your dream? Go after it today and believe that anything is possible!

If You're a Fan of This Book, Please Tell Others . . .

- Write about *Trailer Cash* on your blog, Facebook, Twitter, MySpace, LinkedIn, and other social media sites you frequent.
- Suggest *Trailer Cash* to friends. (Word of mouth endorsements are always the best!)
- When you're in a bookstore, ask them if they carry the book. The book is available through all major distributors, so any bookstore that does not have *Trailer Cash* in stock can easily order it.
- Write a positive review of *Trailer Cash* on www.amazon.com.
- Send my publisher, HigherLife Publishing, suggestions on websites, conferences, and events you know of where this book could be offered. E-mail them at media@ahigherlife.com.
- Purchase additional copies to share as gifts.

Connect With Me . . .

To learn more about *Trailer Cash* please contact me at:

Jamie@trailercash.com

You may also contact my publisher directly:

HigherLife Publishing
400 Fontana Circle
Building 1 – Suite 105
Oviedo, Florida 32765
Phone: (407) 563-4806
Email: media@ahigherlife.com

Are you ready to start generating wealth?

Thinking and dreaming about generating significant wealth is nice, but to experience the fruit of it, you have to take action! Here's a simple way to get started...

Go to our website and sign up! It's **free**—no obligation, and no obnoxious sales pitches.

www.trailercash.com

Let me send you inside information on how to get the real-estate investor training you need. By connecting with me, you can receive advance notice of the exclusive seminars I teach with my husband, Ryan. Plus, you'd get the inside scoop on other opportunities and resources we are developing now.

I don't do mass marketing. So if you are not connected with me, you miss out. It's that simple.

I can't stress enough how important it is after reading this book that you *take action!* I wrote this book to help you. Hopefully something in my story has inspired you to think and dream bigger. Now let's take action—together!

Read what others are saying about our seminars and the information Ryan and I share . . .

No theory. All experiential knowledge! Actually, I liked *everything*.

—*B. Johnson, rated the class 10 out of 10*

Loved the examples and the dialog as well as the question-and-answer sessions.

—*A. Messarra, rated the class 10 out of 10*

I liked everything. The presentation made it easy for us to learn without making costly mistakes. If I can retain/utilize 1/2 of what I've learned, then these three days will definitely enable me to close on a park this year. Of all the seminars I've been to on real-estate investing, this one will help me to achieve my goals and dreams. Now I have the tools and the knowledge to apply all that I have learned and to be successful.

—*W. Holman, rated the class 10 out of 10*

This class was packed with very valuable and usable information with a wide-ranging usability. I was very impressed with Ryan and Jamie Smith. I learned a lot about record gathering. This is where I have been lax in the past, and it has cost me money and grief. Better fact gathering will save and increase my buying power. Thank you for a very enjoyable three days!

—*L. Walston, rated the class 10 out of 10*

I sat in the back of the room in awe of the amount of knowledge Ryan and Jamie Smith possess. I even texted a friend just to let him know how awesome this class is. I really liked how you talked to the students to and from the parks on the tour. Not a single minute went by that you weren't teaching us a valuable principle. We definitely got our money's worth! I'm honored to call you guys my friends!

—N. OSMOND, RATED THE CLASS 10 OUT OF 10

The information was clear and based on working knowledge. They tell you what to do and if problems occur solutions to resolve problems.

—D. JONES, RATED THE CLASS 10 OUT OF 10

I liked *everything!* Ryan and Jamie are the very, very best. Never is there a question about your talent, caring, and compassion. Especially from a guy like me. You have helped me become better in so many ways.

—J. LODGE, RATED THE CLASS 10 OUT OF 10

I appreciate the sharing of turnkey processes and tools for allowing us to become successful in distant markets. Your process driving training is phenomenal. So much information is a bit of a large chunk to swallow but *wow!* Great stuff. Your willingness to share for our success is unforgettable! Thank you, thank you, thank you!

—D. MASON, RATED THE CLASS 10 OUT OF 10

I loved everything. It was an incredibly comprehensive education!

—M. BEVER, RATED THE CLASS 11 OUT OF 10

I liked everything!

—C. MOORE, RATED THE CLASS 10 OUT OF 10

1) I received all of the information required to complete a deal. 2) Enough time included for all questions. 3) Visit to the parks. 4) Ability to record and Ryan's video recording. 5) Ability to receive copies of all materials. 6) Seems like Ryan and Jamie will be willing to provide "support" with other questions during my process.

—T. NIKOLIEV, RATED THE CLASS 10 OUT OF 10

The combination of class instruction and field visits to both owned and non-owned parks. This gives perspective to exactly what types of parks you are looking at (the star rating) relative to what situation you want to end up with. The importance of exit strategies to have in place in case these properties have to be divested. Without a doubt, this class will help me achieve my investment goals.

—*W. LEAKE, RATED THE CLASS 10 OUT OF 10*

I enjoyed the simplicity of the presentation. I understood all the concepts. Ryan and Jamie Smith make you feel like you are their friends, not just students. They seem sincerely interested in making sure you succeed. They did a great job!

—*M. LEAKE, RATED THE CLASS 10 OUT OF 10*

I enjoyed Ryan and Jamie's upfront and honest approach to explaining the business. They are very knowledgeable and do a good job explaining the concepts in a fairly simple way, which makes it easy to understand. I enjoyed their presentation and positive approach to working with their students.

—*T. SWITZER, RATED THE CLASS 8 OUT OF 10*

I loved the openness and transparency. This definitely is the most valuable course we have taken so far. It was great to drive by multiple parks to understand the different levels. I truly appreciated the visit at your park. It is definitely a different mindset for what is fixed in a mobile home vs. single-family home. Really good information to know. The case studies were extremely helpful. Everything was excellent!

—*S. GARCIA, RATED THE CLASS 10 OUT OF 10*

The fact that you are not just teaching, but that you give us every piece we need to succeed. Both Jamie and Ryan are totally honest and are respectful of who they are working with. I feel like this is Christmas and my birthday rolled together with the number of gifts (contracts, videos, forms, etc.) that were given to us. When we follow the system, and *execute*, we will succeed!

—*D. MERIRER, RATED THE CLASS 10 OUT OF 10*

Very thorough and organized. Loved the real-life example and practical information you guys have learned. It's essentially turnkey. We just have to do it. Love all of the resources you've shared (contracts, forms, etc.). Very generous of you guys!

—*R. BURDICK, RATED THE CLASS 10 OUT OF 10*

The step-by-step process of walking us through all procedures. I look forward to jumping in! Thank you Jamie and Ryan. I look forward to a long and prosperous relationship. You are godsend for my sister and I. One love.

—C. BECKFORD, RATED THE CLASS 10 OUT OF 10

Depth of the material presented was exceptional!

—M. MINKOFF, RATED THE CLASS 10 OUT OF 10

I wished I had this training two months ago! We just bought a mobile home park, and we could have done so much better. I want to ask that another mobile home park bootcamp happens so I can continue to sharpen my mobile home park skills.

—C. CAMPISI, RATED THE CLASS 10 OUT OF 10

I liked how Ryan and Jamie covered the whole process from A to Z in investing in mobile home parks. They had solutions or answers for all of our questions. Most of all, I really feel like they gave us very real and honest information that we will use. Ryan and Jamie rock! Thanks!

—J. SHUEY, RATED THE CLASS 9 OUT OF 10

I liked the instructors. They were excited, and knew they material. Teaching the lessons from personal experiences were most helpful in learning the material. Always patient and focused on our questions. I appreciated their effort to help.

—B. TRAVIS, RATED THE CLASS 10 OUT OF 10

The knowledge and experience of instructors.

—M. CHARBONNIER, RATED THE CLASS 9 OUT OF 10

I liked the instructors. I also like the fact that the course includes continuing support. This course was well worth the money.

—G. WOJCIK, RATED THE CLASS 10 OUT OF 10

I loved everything. I could have saved us so much if I could have attended this bootcamp two to three months ago when we were buying our first park.

—N. CAMPISI, RATED THE CLASS 10 OUT OF 10

The ease of understanding for people (like me) who have very little real-estate investing experience. The detail. Your willingness to share everything that has taken you years to learn and refine. Your patience with answering the same question over and over again. Your a phenomenal wealth of knowledge!

—P. JOHNSON, RATED THE CLASS 10 OUT OF 10

A–Z approach. This helped me understand all the nuances of mobile home park considerations and evaluations. Guest speakers, the bus tour, actual examples of deal analysis, due-diligence checklists, review, having copies of all documents are going to help me!

Are you ready to get started? Here's all you have to do—register on my website, and I will get you the information you need to get started!

www.trailercash.com